AUTHORS OBSERVATIONS

Preface:

I started to write the enclosed articles/book out of complete frustration with our politicians in Washington and the money that owns them. As I stated in article 1: "socialist democrats in Congress have no idea how to run this country or a popcorn stand." They are bought and paid for puppets. They are owned by foreign countries, far left political groups, Silicon Valley and billionaires. These politicians have sold their souls for power and money. The problem for our American democracy is they also own the media.

I stated many times in my enclosed articles a quote by **former President Harry S. Truman who said: "You cannot get rich in Washington unless you are a crook."** I cannot quote our former President enough and have referred to his quote many more times in these articles. Because I spent my career in the advertising business I understand to communicate a message properly you need reach and frequency. Reach defines the number of people your message reaches and frequency is the number of times you reach them. Both are essential in communicating your message. Remember many of our politicians have become multi-millionaires while their districts, they supposedly serve are in shambles, especially on the left! While the bought and paid for media say nothing. They are too busy pointing at those they hate like President Trump.

The media was in frenzy when President Trump was impeached for his alleged collusion with Russia although not one vote was changed and it was proven to be a hoax. The selective media, which is a complete joke, said nothing when Trump was exonerated. To this day they still try to label Trump with collusion. Compare this to the Biden family's treatment by the selective media when it has been proven Joe Biden his son Hunter and Joe's brother received millions from China. The main stream media has said nothing! China the killer of humanity continues to gets a pass by now President Biden, the left and the media! Frustration! Frustration! Frustration!

America please understand that the main stream media is owned by anti-God socialists. China created a virus in its laboratories and spread it throughout the world to kill hundreds of thousands of people and the numbers keep growing. These Chinese communist have no believe in God so any and all human atrocities are fair game. The leaders of America should unite and condemn China for these inhumane murders of humanity. China and their products should be boycotted worldwide until they pay trillions to all those infected. Poor countries that have little medical resources and lost loved ones should be paid first.

Let's see if the new Democratic administration confronts China and makes them pay for their evil. Also let's evaluate the main stream media that is supposed to uncover criminal acts of terror and destruction and evaluate their coverage of this evil to humanity. I will unfortunately predict that the bought and paid for media stooges will say nothing unless instructed by the left to do so. The reason for these articles and my complete frustration with the Socialists, Marxists and Communists, further referred to as (SMC), anti-God far left groups is that nothing against the lefts tranny will be reported by the media.

The far left (SMC) have unfortunately great influence in America and our political system. They want to change America into a socialist country void of our Judeo-Christian values, destroy our Constitution and distort our forefather's contributions and history.

Everything that America stands for they will condemn and reposition as evil.

The left has removed God from the classroom, our pledge of Allegiance and from our judicial system. Many on the left say it's your right and okay to kneel for the National Anthem and show no respect to our soldiers and forefathers who died for our country. Now the self-righteous, finger pointer House Judiciary Chairman Jerry Nadler refused to allow the Star Spangled Banner to be played in Congress. One of his donors must have put pressure on him and he folded on his so called principles. This total disrespect to God and country has occurred over many years and is a well thought out plan to destroy America by removing our faith in God. It is a water on stone method of warfare that is very hard to detect in its inception! By the time it has been recognized it has been made into law!

Now to make matters worse the SMC's goal is to implement a complete destruction of our American values by: packing the courts, eliminating the First Amendment Free Speech, Second Amendment removing Americans ability to own guns, making Washington DC a state etc. and they will achieve this by defunding police! This is very disturbing because if history is our teacher these are some of the same tactics used by Hitler when in 1933 he defunded police and had his brown shirts over run Germany.

The worst may be yet to come with the political left supporting the funding of late term and after birth abortions. The left always talks about their love for humanity while strongly supporting and encouraging abortion. Late term and after birth abortions are the killing of innocence babies and the left loudly and aggressively support these murders. Anyone that proclaims to be a lover of God cannot condone this evil. Fifty million plus abortions is America's modern day holocaust. No one with a faith in God can condone this evil! No one and they cannot make excuses to justify this!

The left supports and glorifies Black Lives Matter a terrorist group dedicated to bringing violent socialism to America. As I said in an enclosed article that the name (BLM) is a terrorist organization that disguises their terrorist agenda with their name. From a marketing stand point their name is brilliant and makes people think they are for black people when in reality they are a violent anti American group dedicated to bringing violent change to America. This has been proven many times when they will supply rocks to a demonstration site a day before a demonstration and that is a documented fact. In spite of this many far left politicians sing their praises and some professional athletes donate millions to BLM a terrorist group.

Many democrats are blind and refuse to believe this evil. Ask these blind followers if they have ever witnessed a peaceful BLM demonstration. They are in complete denial when they stated that the 2020 BLM violent demonstrations in cities like Portland, Seattle, Chicago, Minnesota, New York etc. were peaceful. Stores were looted and burned down and lives were destroyed and still many on the left including elected officials refused to condemn this horrible organization and tell the truth. They have sold their souls for power and money!

Yet democrats have become blind to socialist injustice, unless it's the right group and are always pointing at republican voters, who voted for Trump and call them and I am being kind radical and delusional morons! Now to take this insanity to a new and lowest level BLM was nominated for a Nobel Peace Prize! One of the world's most violent terrorists group has been nominated for this, once prestigious prize and our wonderful unbiased main stream media is not outraged. I wonder why? Who owns the media and what is their agenda? If BLM wins the prize I am going to introduce a new name for the Nobel Peace

Prize and call it The Nobel Criminal Prize!

I thank God for people like Tucker Carlson, Hannity and Fox News for standing for American principles. Because of them and guests like Leo Terrell a black activist and former democrat with great uncompromising principles I can at least feel free to vent my frustrations and feel like America still has a chance to survive as the greatest country in the world. Former democrats that have rejected socialism give me hope!

Most clear unbiased Americans understand that the 2020 Presidential election was a complete fraud and Joe Biden won because of it! Google the Robert Epstein 2019 interview with Senator Ted Cruz before it's removed! It clearly states that Silicon Valley has the ability to change votes and was predicted in the interview. It was not done in 2016 to as large a degree because they thought Hillary was a shoe in! When our votes can be manipulated America as we know it is over.

I wrote each article separately, day to day as my frustrations dictated! I felt I wanted to communicate my message in a book framed as articles! Communicating my day to day thoughts to America would hopefully stimulate though for me and my reader. We as Americans must never remain silent when we see our country and values being violated!

Hope you can reflect on American history and our scared principles when reading my articles and voice your disapproval of the socialist left and their assault on America with peaceful but not silent condemnation!

INTRODUCTION TO AMERICAS CHALLENGES FROM FAR LEFT HATERS

Published World Tribune (12/12/19)

I was a leadership, sales and marketing consultant for a number of years and wrote my business book entitled: Create Loyal Customers in an Unloyal World. I would always have my groups, first and foremost, create a Mission Statement. A corporate Mission Statement defines the company's number 1 job priority and it focuses on their customers internally and externally. Every successful and dynamic company must be united and focus on working together to benefit those they serve. Their customers!! That is called leadership 101 "because a house divided against itself cannot stand." Abraham Lincoln knew and coined this phrase in the 1800 hundreds because it cannot be more basic!

The socialist democrats in Congress have no idea on how to run this country or a pop-corn stand. I have always considered the United States as the largest corporation in the world and the democratic socialists, who have no conception of how to run a successful small business, corporation or country, are trying to influence America and determine what success is. The far left socialist trying to pass themselves off as experts in this area is the equivalent of the big con. They believe you give free stuff to everyone and apply huge taxes to any and all successful companies. They have no business or common sense when it comes to creating a successful environment. Yet many of them are being elected to Congress and passing themselves off as experts.

Our politicians always present themselves as representatives of the people and are always looking out for we the people's best interest. Yet the Dems are trying to impeach President Trump for Russian/Ukraine involvement in the 2016 Presidential election. Who has benefited more under this President than many of those Americans in need? Let's look at some of the Presidents many accomplishments-Lowest unemployment for Black-Americans, Hispanic-Americans and Asian-Americans and the highest yearly income growth for average Americans. Also the stock market is at the highest level ever! This means little to nothing to the far left media and those in Congress!

These same politicians are becoming very wealthy

as a result of their collusion with special interest. To verify this fact, I propose that all politicians should be investigated regarding their net worth prior to serving and what they are worth now. How come many of them are millionaires when serving 8 years or more? Be assured many of them do not represent we the people!!! These hypocrites are do nothing finger pointers only interested in power and money! They are there to serve themselves!

Now these far left finger pointers are dedicated and consumed with President Trump's removal from office. The President must be cutting into their profits. Beware America Term limits are the only way to stop this thievery and unfortunately that will never happen as the politicians are the ones who have to approve it!

Charles S. Togias: Author Political Correctness Is Total BS

WASHINGTON'S SELECTIVE CONDEMNERS CONTINUALLY EXPOSED

(12/10/2019)

I want to preface my comments by giving my readers my family background. My father and his family came from Sparta, Greece when my dad was 9 years old. My dad only went to the 7th grade and worked hard his whole life, never taking a penny from anyone. My dad was a no nonsense guy and I have always referred to him as the toughest guy I ever knew! Especially mentally! I remember whenever I got in trouble and tried to blame others, he would always say "I don't care what they did until I first know what you did." I was never allowed to point to others and absolve myself of responsibility and to this day I am thankful for his guidance! I loved my parents and thank them for their guidance.

I have always said that the functional family is the greatest group ever created. They always look internally first before blaming others. They improve the skills and behavior of those they lead. They are role models never asking those they lead to do something they themselves won't do! They discipline non-performance while always showing great love for those they lead!

Now let's look at many of our politicians in Washington, DC, especially our far left finger pointers who are always ready to condemn their rivals while absolving themselves and their party of wrong doing. I refer them as Selective Condemners!

Here are a few examples:

When Joe Biden was V.P., in 2014 his son Hunter Biden was given a consulting job for the Ukraine when he could not speak the language and had no expertise in the job he was hired for. Does anyone know what the Ukraine was given in return? Is it a concern for the selective condemners? No! They are too busy investigating President Trump and his possible Ukraine connection, if there is one. Can you possibly imagine what their response would be if one of Trump's sons was involved in the exact same situation. I for one want Hunter Biden investigated just as I would if any other politician's family was involved!

Regarding these Washington political Selective Condemners Adam Schiff, Jerry Nadler and Maxine Waters I have a couple of questions: How long have they served 'we the people' in politics and what was their net worth when they were first elected? What is it now? Remember when you are pointing your finger you have 3 pointing back. They are the biggest critics of their rival President Trump and his presidency and will never look at themselves or their party. I wonder why?

I have saved the best for last with Crooked Hillary and her destroying 30,000 emails. These selective condemners say nothing. I wonder why she destroyed them and why nothing is being investigated in this matter. Hillary is one of these selective condemners and has been given a complete pass regarding this issue. Selective condemners absolve the actions of their fellow condemners and that is why they have no credibility with anyone with ethics, morals and common sense.

Thomas Jefferson said; "All Tyranny needs to gain a foot hold is for people of good conscience to remain silent."

Charles S. Togias: Author Political Correctness Is Total BS

ISRAEL OUR VALUED FRIEND

(12/12/2019)

I included a chapter entitled: New Religious Alliance in my new book that focuses on Christian and Jews uniting and why it's so vital now for the preservation of our two religions as well as preserving world peace! I want to preface this article by saying that I am a Christian and a supporter of the Jewish people. I feel that many in our global society have condemned the Jewish people for many years. Always looking for reasons to find fault with everything they do and now more than ever it's become a very serious problem.

We have democratic Muslim representatives in Congress verbally attacking Israel and their democratic counter-parts never say a word in defense of Israel. Israel is Americas most trusted ally and these Muslim democratic mud slingers, in Congress are always making derogatory accusations about Israel and the Jewish people in general. America can always count on Israel if we are ever forced to engage in a world conflict.

This worldwide abandonment of Israel became very obvious during the Obama administration with the Iranian deal. It was a huge slap in the face to Israel and put them in great jeopardy. It was very obvious that Obama was anti-Israel and now with these Muslim representatives open condemnation of Israel it's starting to position America as a lukewarm supporter at best.

When we examine Christianity we see that it was originally a Jewish movement. Every writer in the Old and New Testament was Jewish except for Luke who was a Greek doctor. All Jesus Christ's disciples were Jewish. St. Paul, who wrote most of the New Testament, was a devout Jew. Christian salvation is guaranteed through the death and resurrection of Jesus Christ, a Jew. The Christian faith is based on a Jewish messiah. We must always remember this and stay strong with Israel!

I have a theory as to why our Judeo-Christian principles, along with our Constitution which made America the envy of the world are now being attacked. Many far left socialists that seem to have taken over the Democratic Party are secular without a belief in God! Many seculars also believe that our

Constitution is archaic completely outdated with little to no relevance to today. That's why they have taken prayer out of public schools along with the pledge alliance and any reference to Jesus Christ. Muslim can pray! Christians can't! Beware America if we do not stand up for the values that made America the envy of the world we will lose what made us great!

I am very pro-Israel because no group in the history of the world has help mankind more than the Jews. Their ingenuity in science and medicine has help alleviate illness throughout the world. The U.N., which I consider a joke, votes 80% against Israel. These selective condemners (my term) will look under a magnifying glass for Israel's mistakes and say nothing about their great accomplishments.

Remember our Judeo-Christian values and Constitution has made our country and world a better place!

Charles S. Togias: Author Political Correctness Is Total BS

IMMIGRATION AND THE BIG CON!

(12/15/19)

Immigration has become a very heated and controversial topic in our country and it is baffling to me! We, the United States of America have immigration laws as does all other countries in the world. These laws require documentation for all non-U.S. residents. If you are a visitor you are required to have a passport to gain entry. This is known as legal entry and should not be very confusing to anyone from any other part of the world. All countries abide by this process and it's required to insure law, order and the safety of their residents.

A documented system would allow us to keep track of everyone who enters our country which would ensure the safety of all Americans. There are tens of thousands of illegals entering our country and many are threatening the safety of our citizens. So why the controversy when President Trump proposed the building of the wall? I have a theory and its call block voting. If the illegal Hispanics entering our country know that the republicans are against their illegal entry and the democrats are turning a blind eye and not requiring passport enforcement who will they rally behind? Remember an estimated 3 million plus, illegal votes were cast in our 2016 Presidential election! Because of this who do you think those entering our country illegally are going to illegally vote for by the masses? It's called block voting! The socialists' democrats are selling their souls for votes. Surprise! Surprise!!

The wall unquestionably insures the safety of many Americans especially lower income Americans. The democrats are always talking about their love for the masses in our country. Do Nancy Pelosi and Chuck Schumer really feel America is safer without a wall when they were 100% for building the wall, on video just a short time ago? Now they are 100% against the wall! Why? Also if a wall does not insure safety why is Nancy's house surrounded by a wall? When she takes it down I may start to listen to her. Remember our representatives are dedicated to the health, welfare and safety of the American people right? Does any American really believe that? Unfortunately many in Washington practice hypocrisy at its lowest level while becoming rich!

Immigration is an easy problem to fix with strong, decisive leadership. John F. Kennedy said "every man- made problem has a man-made solution." Remember we require every African, Asian, European etc. to have proper documentation to enter our country as we must have to enter their country! Why are they required when those coming through our southern border are not? It's not fair to require some but not all. To have everyone treated the same is called fair and humane!!

Many of our politicians who are reelected in Washington and serve multiple terms become very wealthy. I can't stress this enough. How can this possibly be on their salaries?

President Harry Truman once said: 'You cannot get wealthy in politics unless you're a crook."

Charles S. Togias: Author Political Correctness Is Total BS

CHARLES S. TOGIAS

SELECTIVE CONDEMNERS WASHINGTON STYLE

(1/13/2020)

Article from Political Correctness Is Total BS:
Chapter 1 America's Deception Media Style

When Judge Kavanagh was being scrutinized by Congress before voting him onto the Supreme Court they went back to his high school days and found that he may have had an illicit affair with a teenage girl in high school, which by way has never been proven. He was seventeen she was fifteen. The far left went insane and wanted him, immediately withdrawn. Remember it was high school. I want to preface my following remarks by stating that Kavanagh or anyone else who sexually violates a man, women or child should be prosecuted to the full extent of the law, with no exceptions. The problem I have with their outrage is it's always selective. These selective political condemners rarely if ever investigate themselves or members of their party. That is why I have labeled them as selective condemners.

These Washington phonies are always looking

for anything they can blame on others while always absolving themselves and their party from any wrong doing. So I thought of a biblical verse: "Those that have not sinned cast the first stone." Do you think if all those in Congress were investigated from high school till now they might have some serious explaining to do? To me their condemnation is the equivalent of Dracula accusing and condemning the Red Cross for their methods when taking blood. They are so manipulative when judging their rivals I wonder how they sleep at night.

Just imagine if everyone in Congress was investigated from high school till now what would be uncovered? It would be mind boggling I am sure especially in light of their hypocritical condemnation and perceived outrage with Kavanagh! They hate Kavanagh because they are convinced when voting on the Supreme Court he will vote to overturn Roe vs. Wade.

These far left Washington condemners should not be too quick to point fingers as they are the party of some pretty illicit sexual history. In fact I am sure both parties have many skeletons in their closets. I am very sure that if we went back to all that serve in Congress high school days the skeletons would need a huge, oversized plantation not closet! Remember when pointing at others you have 3 fingers pointing back!

Charles S. Togias: Author Political Correctness Is Total BS

ABORTION/ ABORTIONOLICS LEGALIZATION IS AMERICA'S MODERN DAY HOLOCAUST

(1/23/2020)

I know many women feel it is their body to do with what they want but along with a body goes a brain. Purposely eliminating the life of an otherwise healthy infant is demonic especially when there are so many easy ways to prevent a pregnancy. These helpless infants do not have a say in their future and as a result are being slaughtered. Fifty million abortions is America's holocaust. Abortion in America has become very controversial and that is why I included it in my book, 4th edition: **Political Correctness Is Total BS**.

Many on the far left go so far as believing and promoting that late term abortions is within the woman's rights. Some even believe that after birth abortions are within those rights. The abortion rights people believe it is a women's right issue and not a right to life issue. I did believe that it was both until I came to my senses!!

The legalization of abortion is very controversial in itself. In 1973 the Supreme Court legalized abortion with Roe vs. Wade. The court's decision was based on a vague right to privacy not spelled out in the Constitution. The Supreme Court was legalizing social policy and exceeding its authority as interpreter of the law. The central issue at hand is whether the live child in the womb has Constitutional rights. The Supreme Court decided they did not.

We saw how violent the far left supporters of the woman's right to choose can become when Judge Kavanagh was appointed to the Supreme Court by President Trump. Those on the left went insane which is very common when they are in disagreement. The Judge was called every vial name and accused of crimes dating back to high school. This was all orchestrated by the left because they knew the judge was against keeping abortions legal.

Their hysterical outrage did not surprise me because they become very violent when confronted by another point of view. I find this morbid but almost comical because the left is always talking about their love for humanity. Disagree with them on these issues and see how violently they will attack, while always talking about their love for humanity. The left is the epitome of hypocrisy and violence!

Getting back to the subject at hand, abortion and how to present this to the American people to help them arrive at a moral and ethical conclusion. My recommendation would be to show the entire procedure on television. Similar to how the A.S.P.C.A shows animal cruelty. I love animals especially dogs and I am driven to tears when I see how many are treated so inhumanly. If we created a similar type video and described the entire abortion procedure from its beginning to its conclusion even to the point of discarding the fetal remains I want to see how people would react. Some may say that showing an abortion on television is barbaric. If it is too barbaric to show it may just be too barbaric to perform. When you stop a baby from breathing that means they were alive and you killed them. Period!! Remember the more information we get the more confident and comfortable we are in our decisions!

Fifty million abortions is a national disgrace, and I was not even dogmatic on the abortion issue until I research these figures. With 50 million abortions we have no idea who has been destroyed and if they had lived what they may have contributed to

mankind. It is America's modern day holocaust!!
Charles S. Togias: Author Political Correctness Is Total BS

WASHINGTON, DC MAFIA

Published World Tribune (2/13/2020)

I want to focus on what is happening in our nation's capital or otherwise referred to as the swamp. To get the reader's attention I included the word "Mafia" in the title, to call attention to this mindless political travesty. Before we go any further I want to apologize to those in the Mafia and their leaders. We know they operate with much more dignity and respect for each other than many of these far left Washington politicians. I did not in any way try to compare the Mafia with these horrible finger pointing elitists. My goal was trying to call attention to this terrible situation because the main stream media will not. The political left, their leaders and the main stream media are one! Thank God for Fox News!!

When I see what is happening with the far left politicians in Washington and their continued attacks on President Trump I am in disbelief. A very simple example is how outraged democratic leaders like Nancy Pelosi, Adam Schiff, Nadler and their many far left followers are when accusing President Trump of colluding with the Ukraine to undermine the election and yet say nothing about Joe Biden and his son Hunter. With the help of the main stream media the far left pointers are given credibility.

Joe Biden's son Hunter was paid millions of dollars to be a consultant in the Ukraine for a company/product he knew nothing about and could not speak the language. To make matters even worse Biden is accused of having the Ukrainian prosecutor fired who was going to investigate this political travesty and this was done while he was Vice-President. Yet the political hoodlums serving in Congress never have said a word condemning this atrocity. They are blindly focused on trying to prove that President Trump was pressuring Ukraine to investigate this matter. I said in my book Political Correctness is Total BS that if Mr. Trump did not urge the Ukrainian's to look into this matter it would be a dereliction of duty. We as American citizens are letting these political hoodlums live by a completely different standard while they would persecute American citizens and their rivals for doing the same.

Since so many of them are always pointing at their rival's and accusing them of misdeeds I felt a need to evaluate their morals and ethics with a very simple suggestion: All members of the House and

Senate have their net worth investigated from what it was prior to taking office and what it is currently. I believe the numbers would be staggering. If they have nothing to hide they should welcome the inquiry. After that investigation has been completed I want to see how many of them will be able to point their fingers at anyone.

Question: What was Bernie Sanders career in civilian life and net worth prior to getting into Politics?

President Truman said: "You can't get rich in Washington unless you are a crook."

Again, my sincere apologies to members of the Mafia for comparing them to many of the Washington insiders!! These insiders talk about their integrity while they lie and cheat to achieve their agenda. Comparing any group to these swamp rats is unfair!!
Charles S. Togias: Author Political Correctness Is Total BS

TERRORISM

(3/2/2020)

In the Terrorism chapter of my book: Political Correctness Is Total BS I came up with an idea on how to eliminate worldwide Terrorism without firing a shot. When researching the terrorist's mentality I thought it would be impossible to successfully reason with this type of distorted mindset and I was frustrated as you will sense when you read this chapter. These Muslim terrorist will never stop killing innocent men, women and children because they think their God instructs them to do so no matter what we say or do using conventional wisdom. Remember a great many Muslim Fundamentalist, believe the killing of non-Muslims regardless of age, will bring them immortality and to argue with this type of insanity is futile. So I thought of a John F. Kennedy quote as I often do: "Every man made problem has a man-made solution" and tried to devise a well thought out simple plan that would resonate with the most hateful terrorist and end this senseless global slaughter.

I wanted to use simple logic rather than to continue to endorse more military aggression to counteract terrorism. I wanted to save lives on both sides and stop this demonic senseless human slaughter! Our current military strategy has only created martyrs and increased the terrorist resistance as well as taken the lives of many American soldiers as well as innocent Americans at home. Instead of helping to alleviate the problem we've compounded it while spending billions of dollars worldwide.

My simple 3 step approach:

1. We should create a technology that would coat all of our weapons with pork residue. Every bullet, bomb, piece of scrap metal every weapon that we take into combat should be coated. We will never produce another weapon or take a weapon into combat without the pork coating. It's not having a spray used to coat each bullet it is developing a technology that will coat every military weapon from this day forward with pork residue. America will never take a weapon into combat again that is not coated!

2. Our military will create a video that will describe the entire process from the development of the pig residue to that actual coating of the weapons. This will make it perfectly clear to

friend and foe that we have the technology and have implemented it.

3. We will have our field commanders meet with our allies to make them fully aware of our new technology. They will present our strategy in a way that will encourage the world leaders to understand that we are striving for a peaceful resolution that will save lives. We will then leave the middle which will save billions of dollars and save the lives of American soldiers!

My idea, if implemented is the exact opposite of what Washington under the Obama administration did when they gave $150 billion dollars to Iran. Iran is the main sponsor of terrorism in the world and when they received the money their citizens were chanting death to America and death to Israel. You never try to appease a horrible dictatorship, such as Iran, by bribing them!

In conclusion: You use conventional wisdom when dealing with conventional people and unconventional wisdom when dealing with unconventional people!! We will also share our new technology with Israel!

Charles S. Togias: Author Political Correctness Is Total BS

ABORTION-AMERICA'S MODERN DAY HOLOCAUST

(3/7/2020)

Abortion is very controversial and that's why I included it in my book: Political Correctness Is Total BS. Each side of the abortion issue is very passionate in its beliefs. On one side, those who support abortion feel it's a woman's right to do what she wants with her body. On the other side, those opposed feel abortion is murder. The problem is compounded because the far left pro abortionist will never listen to the other point of view.

Many pro abortionist object to any limitations on abortion even late term abortions. They believe very strongly that it is a women's body therefore her right to choose. As I stated, in my book, along with a body goes a brain. If concerned with becoming pregnant there are easy ways to prevent a pregnancy. Pro-abortionists feel that abortion is a freedom issue and not a right to life issue. I think the problem is that it may be both.

Many anti-abortionists feel it is a religious issue and refer to biblical passages to make their point.

These biblical passages support their point of view. They feel the live fetus in the womb is a child and should be protected. Many anti-abortionists refer to Jeremiah 1:5 (Old Testament) which says: "Before I formed you in the womb I knew you, and before you were born I consecrated you." This statement is very powerful especially for those who believe the Bible is the living word of God!

The legalization of abortion is very controversial in itself. In 1973, the Supreme Court legalized abortion with Roe vs. Wade. The court's decision was based on a vague right of privacy not spelled out in the Constitution. The Supreme Court was legislating social policy and exceeding its authority as interpreter of the law. The central issue at hand is whether the live child in the womb has Constitutional rights. The Supreme Court decided they did not.

There is an old saying that a little knowledge is a dangerous thing and that is absolutely true, especially in the case of abortion. For this reason **we should provide society with as much information as possible on this issue and to do so, my recommendation would be to show abortions on television**. If the fetus comes out a mass of tissue, the pro-abortions will win over the majority of public opinion. If on the other hand, the fetus comes out developed with arms, legs, fingers etc. then the anti-abortionist will gain public support. Show the entire procedure from the beginning to the discarding of the fetus. Some people may say that showing an abortion on television is barbaric and I say if it is too barbaric to show it may be to barbaric to perform.

I have never seen an abortion and do not know all the facts. I do know that at present if the baby comes out alive it will be destroyed. That is the main reason late term abortions must be shown to all Americans so they can decide if that is humane or completely barbaric. Show the entire process to all Americans so when they make a decision they will be completely informed.

If we applied the same logic to the death penalty and in 40 plus years 50 million convicts were executed there would be a national outcry and rightly so especially by the far left abortion rights crew. It would not matter how horrific their crimes they would be in a frenzy. But the killing of innocent babies in their mother's womb is completely justified.

We may have aborted some babies that if they lived may have achieved greatness as scientists or humanitarians benefiting all of humanity. For me 50 million abortions is more than a protest its wholesale murder. The Killing of an innocent human being is beyond barbaric and fifty million innocent babies being slaughtered is demonic!! Wake up America!!

Fifty million abortions is America's modern day holocaust!

Charles S. Togias: Author Political Correctness Is Total BS

WAKE UP AMERICA

Published World Tribune (3/12/2020)

The way the far left and media seem to be rejoicing over the collapse of the stock market due to the coronavirus confirms without a doubt, the radical Dems and their partners in the main stream media would rather have President Trump fail/impeached even if it meant his success would improve the lives of all Americans. This is a hatred/vendetta that the vast majority of responsible Americans including myself, cannot comprehend. Only the radical left hate like that. They are the true enemy within because Russia could not want America's destruction more!

I believe that if our country suffered another major depression similar to the crash of 1929 under President Trump, I have no doubt, the far left and media would be cheering. They could care less about the welfare of the average American they just want him out. My question is could this hysteria by the radical socialists, which have taken over the democratic party, lead to another civil war in our country? I feel the possibilities are certainly there not only because of their evil vendetta but because they are supported by the Main stream media who gleefully communicates and supports their hatred.

I have never witnessed a situation such as this and did not think it was possible in America. I had no idea elements of our population were capable of this. The far left politicians lie and the main stream media swear to it. As I have stressed throughout my book: **Political Correctness is Total BS** in the history of America I had no idea this was possible because I was under the false impression that all Americans realized that America was and is the greatest country and the envy of the world.

I have a recommendation to help bring America back. First Term limits! I believe under the current environment, if not corrected, we as a nation will continually decline. The problem is the good old boys in Washington will never vote in favor of it. It's like a Mafia boss voting to take away his money and power and go back on the street. The special interest money alone would cost them a fortune. America don't be deceived it's all about their power and money! They are there to benefit themselves not 'we the people'!! Be 100% sure of that!! So if possible we should investigate starting a class action law suit against these villains. I know presently, under our laws and Constitution it's not a possibility and if not change the law. Remember the far left in Washington want to change and eliminate the Electoral College for their benefit so my idea is create a class action law-suit, by changing the law, to force term limits to benefit 'we the people' from these self-serving hypocrites.

I want to end this article by expressing my grave concerns with our so called "unbiased" main stream media. They have become anything but unbiased and main stream. They are now far left stream. They appeal to a far-left group whose intentions are to destroy our democratic republic and change everything our founding fathers and our country has stood for. We are the envy of the world and that is why so many millions of immigrants risk their lives to live here. If this does not change dramatically and we continue to be a hopelessly divided country against an elected President our ability to function as a democratic democracy may be in jeopardy and a civil war may be in our future. Don't laugh if things don't change it could happen!

Be 100% assured of one thing: The far left Washington insiders are not serving "We the people" they only serve themselves and their wallets!! That is a proven fact because of their dramatic increase in net worth while "serving we the people" in office! Example: Bernie Sanders never had high paying job in his career and now, serving in Political Office is worth millions. There are many more examples! Check it out!!

Wake up America before it's too late!!!!

Charles S. Togias: Author Political Correctness Is Total BS

MENTALITY: LAWYER VS. BUSINESS AND WASHINGTON, DC

(3/21/2020)

Lawyers have what I describe as a process or procedural mentality. The longer it takes them to solve a problem the more they profit. They defend the process because they have been taught that the justice system allows them to withhold value evidence if it allows their clients to go free. Actual example: In my book: **Political Correctness Is Total BS, 4TH edition** I presented a judge with a hypothetical situation and wanted to know his opinion. I defined the situation by saying he was presiding over a trial where a man was accused of shooting another man, in the head and killing him. I stated that during the trial a video tape was put on his desk showing that the crime he was being accused of actually happened. I also said that the video showing the crime did not go through proper procedure and therefore was inadmissible and as a result the perpetrator was found innocent and went free. I asked him if that was justice and without hesitation he said 100%. The judge stated that is how our system works! If that is the way our system works that means to me our system of justice can be manipulated and is broken.

Lawyers take this procedural mentality to Washington D.C. while they serve in Congress so they can always justify their actions. Whether they are pointing at their rivals or making millions working with special interest groups. I am emphasizing this point because Washington DC is made up of lawyers and it is my opinion that this is what is destroying America's credibility. Internally and externally!!

Business people on the other hand are what I describe as being outcome focused because the quicker they solve the problem the more money they make. In my opinion this is one of the main reasons the Washington insiders and their partner's in the media hate President Trump. President Trump gets things done immediately! At times he can be very crude in his tweets and can be easily criticized on the way he addresses those who disagree with him like the far left politicians and main stream media do every day. But what is important to me is he gets things done. In fact it was the main stream media and political left that got me to become a big fan of our President. I was not a fan prior.

I was a General Sales Manager at an NBC affiliate

in Syracuse, New York many years ago. I kept my job for 15 plus years because we made and exceeded our monthly and yearly projections by being outcome focused. We were successful because the clients we served benefited greatly from our advertising expertise. Talk is cheap and many big talkers in Washington become millionaires while the districts they serve are in shambles. I have always believed that success is based solely on meeting and exceeding projections for yourself and those you employ/serve. Example: If I was elected to serve a district and the people, who elected me, were not enriched by my decisions and leadership I should resign and never profit!!

That is leadership 101!!

Conclusion: Americans better start evaluating every politician and evaluate their successes and more importantly their districts success. Everything else is meaningless! After all they pledge to serve "we the people." Let's start to encourage those that have successful business backgrounds to represent "we the people" and replace the self-serving talkers with doers!!!

Charles S. Togias: Author Political Correctness Is Total BS

UNPARALLELED HATRED FROM OUR FAR LEFT RULING CLASS...

Published World Tribune (3/28/2020)

The following is a word by word quote, Chapter 1, from my book Political Correctness Is Total BS.

"I now know without a doubt the radical Dems would rather have President Trump fail/impeached even if it meant his success would improve the lives of humanity than having him succeed and win for America and the world. That is a hatred that most responsible people cannot comprehend! Only the radical left can hate like that. If our country suffered another major depression like in 1929 under President Trump I have no doubt the left would be cheering! They could care less about the average Americans well-being they just want him out! Could this hysteria by the radical socialist lead to another civil war in our country? I feel the possibilities are certainly there. There is an old saying and I apply it to the Washington insiders: "Those that cannot do teach." I am not applying this to most teachers just Washington. In the history of America I have never witnessed a situation such as this. I had no idea elements of our population were capable of this."(Featured in Chapter 1)

I wrote this in my book, many months before the coronavirus scare and the eventual market collapse. This is why I have great concerns with the coronavirus situation in America and how it is affecting our country, especially the average American and the stock market. I am not saying that Americans should not be greatly concerned with the virus I just have little faith in our politicians, especially those on the left in complete hysteria over this situation and their self-serving agendas.

Recently I was discussing the coronavirus situation with a doctor friend of mine and he brought up some interesting facts. He said the flu in America last year killed 37,000 plus Americans. The doctor also indicated that around one percent of those that get the flu parish from it. That is slightly under those who die from the coronavirus. The doctor wondered, as I do, why there is such hysteria over an illness where the average person will fully recover from this illness? Could it be fueled by the Washington far left, Trump hating, finger pointers? I do not trust anything they say or do because I find that the reason for their outrage is always self-serving!

When I start to look into what is happening to America with this epidemic and review the Washington insiders hysteria as well as their partners in the main stream media regarding President Trump I have real questions and concerns. If the stock market continues to have record breaking declines could that lead to a 1929 depression and if so is that their goal? America is closing down as most Americans are not working and as a result most businesses are closed. I want my above 1929 prediction to be wrong!

We should also look at China's possible involvement. President Trump has been continually out negotiating China and they are very upset about it. Many believe that China's bio lab's released the virus worldwide to get back at America and Trump! Whether this is true or not it is very possible yet is never condemned or investigated by the left and ought to be. It's only Trump's fault!

I have a great love for America but have great concerns for the far left politicians and their partners in the media as their goal is to destroy the America that we love. They are corrupt and will resort to anything to compromise our President. I pray that the coronavirus will be over very soon. I also pray that Americans will understand that there are some really demented people in our country that are self-serving socialists that want to change America and will do anything even to bankrupt our country to achieve their goal! Have an open mind and don't fall for the far left con artists!!

God Bless America!!

Charles S. Togias: Author Political Correctness Is Total BS

CHINA'S UNDECLARED WORLD WAR IN THE FORM OF A PANDEMIC

(4/09/2020)

As of today, April 9th, 2020 there have been over 90,000 deaths due to the coronavirus worldwide and the numbers just keep multiplying. Is it the result of China making a concerted effort to spread this virus that has its origins in China? Is it pay back for tariffs and loss of revenue due to many American companies who had left our country and now are returning as a result of China being completely out negotiated by President Trump and his administration? When contemplating my theory let's not forget that many large American companies from China were returning to America and our stock market was booming under Trump before this pandemic!

Let's look at the players: China is a communist country and has little regard for anything other than their world dominance. They have dominated the world industrial market and as a testament to this we, in the past, have had many American companies leave

America and go to China. Our former Presidents and their administrations were not masters in negotiations and were not able to compete with Chinas business enticements. Then China was introduced to President Trump! Remember President Trump is not a lawyer he is a very successful businessman who has made a living on being a great negotiator.

Could this cause China to spread this virus to the world as payback? It has limited the growth of our stock market and shut America down! If so this is so horrendous I feel China could be capable of anything! The disregard for human life at this magnitude is beyond what normal, peace loving people can comprehend. This is a Hitler mentality! To even think that this could be a possibility is frightening and I am sorry to say I cannot rule it out!

The reason for my concern is in business timing is everything. America was booming under Trump as our stock market was at an all-time high and most of our businesses were growing at a record breaking pace. As I stated above America for the first time ever was getting our industries to return to America from China. In the past they were all going the other way. To add to this there are some in our country who wanted America to fail under President Trump that may also be part of the conspiracy and if so it would not surprise me. In fact, if some of those that possess the power and political influence were involved it would be par for the course.

I said in my book: Political Correctness Is Total BS, 4TH edition that the political left would welcome a depression for America than see President Trump succeed! Their hatred for President Trump supersedes their perceived commitment to serve "we the people" that they took an oath to serve and that adds to my suspicions! Many of the far left in powerful positions and in Washington are dedicated to changing America, our Constitution and everything that has made America the envy of the world. They have no common sense and will resort to anything to destroy America!

Beware America of China and the political Trump haters with their evil intentions. They will resort to anything to achieve their agenda: To remove Trump!

Charles S. Togias: Author Political Correctness Is Total BS

MAIN STREAM MEDIA AND THEIR FAR LEFT SUPPORTER'S AGENDA OF COLLUSION AND DECEPTION

(4/20/2020)

When I see the way the main stream media and the far left politicians are always attacking everything that President Trump and his administration do without ever complimenting his victories and successes it frightens me. Example when unemployment of Blacks, Hispanics and Asian Americans went to an all-time low they said little to nothing. When the stock market went to all-time highs they would focus on other areas they could find that were negative. They avoided the victories in unemployment and the market to find any areas that were negative! They hate President Trump beyond anything I thought was possible and want him to fail!

When his predecessor President Obama was in office they did the exact opposite. They never focused or even mention his very questionable anti-American decisions. Let's look at how the crooked politicians and main stream media treated the Obama administration and judge if they were fair.

In the first chapter of my book: **Political Correctness Is Total BS**, 4th edition, I give some examples. Collusion- Dems and media say that Russia interfered with our 2016 election although not one vote, by their own admission was ever changed. If that is collusion how come the estimated 3 million illegals that voted was not collusion? I wonder if it was not considered collusion because of who they voted for.

Obama was a member of Reverend Wrights Church for 22 years and his character is never challenged by the main stream media. Reverend Wright should have been a topic of controversy because of his anti-sematic and anti-white messages and the media remained silent. Remember this is the same media who labeled President Trump as anti- Semitic even though his daughter converted to Judaism marrying her Jewish husband and raising their daughter Jewish. Obama was never labeled as anti-Semitic??? Also Obama was friends with anti-American Bill Ayers and the main stream media remained silent! I wonder if our media would have attacked Trump if he was involved in these situations? I never heard a word regarding Obama from the now righteous Nancy Pelosi or Chuck Schumer.

These atrocities of media and political deception reach an all-time absurdity with the Obama administration giving 150 billion dollars to Iran, the number one supporter of worldwide Terrorism while their citizens were in the streets chanting "death to Israel and death to America" and our main stream media remained silent!! What would have been the media's reaction if President Trump was involved and not Obama? This is well beyond dereliction of duty, by the media, it is an agenda designed to overturn the voter's perceptions and assure their desired outcome in the 2020 election. The main stream media is bastardizing themselves to remove a duly elected President from a second term because of their hatred!

This situation with the media and far left may be similar to what happened in Cuba to allow a horrible tyrant like Fidel Castro to rule. Castro was a horrible leader and murdered those that opposed him. That's why so many Cubans crossed shark infested water and risk their and their families' lives to come to America. I have great compassion for the Cubans and do not want to see this type of horrible situation happen in America! If socialism and communism is so good and America and its traditions and values are so bad how come we never see anyone crossing shark infested waters going from Florida to Cuba?

News flash to our main stream media: You are supposed to report the news in an unbiased manner not censor it to fit your agenda. News censorship is what happens in Communist countries.

Wake up America time may be running out!

Charles S. Togias: Author Political Correctness Is Total BS

AMERICA'S MEDIA AND FAR LEFT POLITICIANS ARE A TEAM FOCUSED ON TRUMP'S REMOVAL

(4/25/2020)

The main stream media is in the pocket of the political left and their wealthy supporters so Americans better wake up and understand the importance of the 2020 election for themselves and more importantly their children. The political far left and their far left secular supporters want to change America and everything that made us the envy of the world. Remember people came from all over the world for religious freedom and opportunity! Not handouts.

They are always attacking President Trump for whatever he does and never said anything about President Obama. Obama was the most unqualified person ever to occupy the White House and made decisions that were beyond illogical. Obama was a community organizer and had no experience with local, state or national matters. Obama's resume before he was President included: member of Reverend Wrights very questionable church for 22 years. A church that from all indications was anti-sematic. I could not have stayed in that church 22 minutes! Obama stayed for 22 years and the main stream media never made an issue of it.

America under Obama gave Iran, the worst and most dangerous terrorist country since Germany under Adolph Hitler, $150 billion and the right to create an atomic weapon. Still the main stream media said nothing. Obama and his administration did this while the Iranians were in the street chanting death to Israel and death to America. The main stream media did not only look the other way they accused Trump of being anti-sematic even though his daughter married a Jewish man and are raising her in the Jewish faith.

Many politicians have become very wealthy while supposedly serving "we the people" in Washington and the media never questions it if they are of the right political persuasion. If you really want to know if politics is profitable check out Bernie "never had a real job" Sanders and Obama's net worth before and now into their political careers!! Former President

Harry Truman said: 'you can't get rich in Washington unless you're a crook."

The main stream Media will not investigate the Washington left. Can you imagine what the main stream media's reaction would be if Trump was involved in this deception?

The media was in a frenzy regarding the accusations that Russia and later when that was dispelled Ukraine's supposedly involvement in the 2016 election in helping Trump become President. Yet the media has said very little about Hunter Biden being paid millions by the Ukraine to be a consultant for them even though he could not speak the language and had no knowledge of the business he was consulting. Joe Biden was V.P. when this occurred and has never had to answer for it. Instead the press focused on President Trump and accused him of pressuring Ukraine's President Volodymyr Zelensky to investigate this matter. Also how about reports of Hillary Clinton's involvement in Russia obtaining uranium and then Russia putting millions into the Clinton Foundation! The press has totally back off on these accusations!! I wonder why? All I know is she, by her own video admission, was dead broke a few years ago and is now worth over $100 million!

Do you think that if President Trump's son was involved in this consulting scandal the main stream media might react differently? I was a Leadership, Sales and Marketing consultant for many years and I actually had to know the business I was consulting and the language! My father and family were not in politics!

Listen to me America-How many of your sons and daughters would ever have the opportunity to make millions without knowing anything about what you were consulting?? Washington politicians took an oath to work for "we the people." Do you really think those on the left with their self-serving agenda care about us??

Now we have the coronavirus. Many of those in the media are blaming Trump for the current situation. They said little about Black, Hispanic and Asian unemployment being at an all-time low and that the stock market being the highest ever. Remember when the stock is at an all-time high that means jobs for Americans. The Washington left and the media want Trump to fail even if that means Americans will suffer. I continue to say that I am totally convinced that if under President Trump we had another major depression they on the left would be cheering. Remember if the stock continued to grow at the rate it was growing Trump was a shoo-in 2020! The left and media would never allow that and that has only increased my suspicions.

Who cause this world wide pandemic and why? Were China and the political left and their wealthy supporters behind it? Did China want revenge for all the tariffs and their loss of American businesses? China has out negotiated every President for many years and finally they met their match. President Trump was a very skilled negotiator for most of his life and unlike Obama made a very good living at it prior to being elected to office. Trump was over qualified in this area and China took a beating dollar wise!

Please believe me America for the media to not emphasize any of Trump's many accomplishments and only focus on what they can spin says a lot about what they think of the American people. They think we are stupid and they can con us into thinking their BS is credible! The far left politicians lie and the media swear to it!

Remember America if President Trump found the cure for cancer the mainstream media and their far-left partners in Washington would spin it and crucify Trump for taking credit and would position it as Obama's victory. They are trying to change America to a socialist country and will do or say anything to discredit and remove Trump! They will and have lied and misrepresented the facts to accomplish their evil goal!

News Flash to our main stream: You are supposed to report the news in an unbiased manner not censor it. News censorship is what happens in Communist countries!!

Charles S. Togias: Author Political Correctness Is Total BS, 4TH edition

THE EVILS OF SOCIALISM/COMMUNISM (VOID OF GOD)

(5/14/2020)

I want to start my article by giving my reader the Webster dictionary's definition of communism. Communism is a theory advocating elimination of private property. A system which goods are owned in common and are available to all as needed. A doctrine based on revolutionary Marxian Socialism and Marxism-Leninism that was the official ideology of the U.S.S.R. a total system of government in which a single authoritarian party controls state owned means of production.

The government controls the wealth that's why those in the Russian government are so wealthy and those they, supposedly serve, are starving. This may be slowly happening in our country. Hillary Clinton is worth tens of millions after Russia put huge amounts of money in her Clinton Foundation. This might be a coincidence but this was after she worked with Russia on them receiving uranium. Remember she is on video prior to these events saying she was "dead broke." Please look up her VIDEO.

Hillary Clinton is among many in Washington that has become very wealthy such as: Barack Obama Bernie Sanders and many, many others. Then I recently heard a democratic Senator, who is always attacking Trump, talk about his outrage on how the Trump administration was handling the pandemic and how it would negatively affect the American people. I was with a friend so he looked up his financial history. In 2014 this righteous Senator was worth 1.45 million and in 2020 is worth 12 million. We have many ways to verify those that serve in Washington and check out their financial history before and after being elected. Don't be conned many are only there to serve themselves! I have labeled them P.B.M-Politicians Becoming Millionaires. Remember Former President Truman's quote: "You can't get rich in Washington unless you're a crook."

Also remember President Trump does not take a salary!!

These are just a very few examples how those in Washington talk a good game and are there to personally profit from the decisions they render! That's a reason I am outraged by their condemnation of a decorated war hero and 3 star general like Flynn.

He is consistently attacked by these phonies and was jailed. Most of these Washington elitist's have never spent a day defending their country in battle only making money off the conflicts that "we the people" have to engage in!

The problem as I see it is many of those in Washington especially on the socialist left have abandoned what was the core values of our democracy Our Constitution and our Judeo-Christian values and principles. I am going to end this article with some quotes designed to stimulate thought and bring clarity to what our founding fathers and other dedicated Americans goals were for all Americans!

"Our Constitution was made only for a moral and religious people. It is wholly inadequate to the government of any other." John Adams (2nd President of USA)

"I predict future happiness for Americans if they prevent the government from wasting the labors of the people under the pretext of taking care of them." Thomas Jefferson (President USA)

President John F. Kennedy was once quoted at a 1962 Noble Prize dinner at the White House:

"I think this is the most extraordinary collection of talent and human knowledge that has ever been gathered together at the White House, with the possible exception of when Thomas Jefferson dined alone."

Again Thomas Jefferson: "All tyranny needs to gain a foothold is for people of good conscience to remain silent."

Beware America the far left Politicians and their secular money supporters want to change our country into a socialist anarchy. They have removed our pledge allegiance from schools, our national anthem, Ten Commandments or reference to God from public buildings. American students have lost the right to pray in school. America was the envy of the world because of our religious liberties.

I am ending this article with another Thomas Jefferson quote:

"I tremble for my country when I reflect that God is just; that his justice cannot sleep forever."

Charles S. Togias: Author Political Correctness Is Total BS

VERY EASY SOLUTION TO END CORONAVIRUS SHUT DOWN

(5/15/2020) (See end of article)

I believe, without a doubt, that the Chinese Communist Virus, known worldwide as the coronavirus was purposely manufactured to prevent America from its greatest economy and growth ever. We must all remember that we had the lowest Black, Hispanic and Asian American unemployment ever. Our stock market growth as well as our economy was on a record breaking pace and if this continued all hard working Americans and their families would have benefited greatly. If this was allowed to continue President Trump and his administration would have been recognized as achieving economic success beyond what any other administration could have envisioned.

To many secular far left billionaires and their Washington political left supporters in Congress this was beyond anything they could tolerate. This would have disrupted their socialist plan to change America. They are dedicated to changing everything that has made America the greatest democratic republic ever formulated. This virus was their war against America! If America's economy continued as it was headed they would have to endure another 4 years of the Trump administration!

When the video describing Dr. Judy Mikovits concerns with how the virus developed worldwide and the vaccines developed years earlier to prevent the virus was aired the video was immediately taken off of YouTube! In fact in her book co-authored by Kent Heckenlively she expresses real concerns with Dr. Fauchi's and his credibility. Try and see the video or buy her book to come to your own conclusions. You cannot view the video as the video has been removed as well as the book from all major book stores. Information stimulates thought and the lack of information only causes confusion. What is the left afraid of?

Dr. Kashid Buttar, another doubter actually referred to Dr. Fauchi as a fraud. I have no idea if any of these accusations are true I just would like to have all the pros and cons referring to all these physicians investigated to prevent more hardship and keep everyone worldwide safe. I love all of humanity and want love, peace and everyone healthy and able to provide for themselves and family.

Ten of thousands of people have died due to this virus worldwide and if it was man made to disrupt our economy it is demonic. If the vaccines previously developed will continue to cause additional victims worldwide that's Hitler type warfare and should be exposed immediately. Information stimulates thought and thought stimulate ideas. I have no trust in the secular far left as they will do anything to achieve their secular, far left agenda to change America and our Judeo-Christian culture.

My solution to get an immediate resolution to defeat this pandemic is very simple:

1. Until America becomes fully employed no politician will be paid one penny! I mean FULLY employed from career workers to day laborers. If Americans don't get paid they don't either.

2. All Chinese products never again will be permitted to be imported here until China pays America/Americans trillions of dollars for the hardship they have caused. I would also recommend every other country who has suffered deaths and loss of jobs to do the same.

Charles S. Togias: Author Political Correctness Is Total BS

CHARLES S. TOGIAS

AMERICA'S TRIALS AND TRIBULATIONS BECAUSE OF THE FAR LEFT SOCIALIST DOCTRINE/ INVASION!

(5/20/2020)

When I see what is happening in Washington with our politicians I am in disbelief. It's contrary to everything I have taught and been taught. Leaders build unity because "a house divided against itself cannot stand." Now they want to vote to get rid of the Electoral College because it will benefit them. I have a better idea, I propose they vote for term limits and benefit "We the People" that they supposedly serve.

I spent my career in sales and sales management and was fortunate enough to work for WSYR, an NBC affiliate located in Syracuse, New York. Over my career we were owned by S.I. Newhouse, later Katz Communication (largest rep firm in the world) and then employee owned by New City Communications. All

79

great companies are dedicated to their employee's growth and success and they were. They provided us the best corporate trainers in the world. For example-Herb Cohen, who negotiated with Iran for the release of our embassy personal, trained us in negotiations. At the time he was considered the best negotiator in the world.

After leaving the media business, with my expertise in hand, I became a Corporate Leadership, Sales and Marketing Consultant with clients in the U.S. and Australia! My previous book: Create Loyal Customers in an Unloyal World describes my Leadership, Sales and Marketing system from beginning to end in its exact order. I have always believed that great companies emulate the functional family. The functional family is the most efficient and effective group ever. Because they love, teach and discipline those they lead. I have always considered Washington D.C. the largest corporation in the world and am horrified by what I see. This is the reason I wrote my book.

The above was written on the back cover of my book: Political Correctness Is Total BS!

To continue to voice my concerns: The far left democrats and their partners in the main stream, delusional media, want to bring President Trump down even if it means changing everything America stands for. I could not have predicted that the left would be so corrupt and devious that they would deny Communist China's participation in the coronavirus that have killed and will continue to kill hundreds of thousands worldwide. They are blaming the virus and those Murdered by the Chinese communists on Trump and giving the communist in China a pass. This is the equivalent of excusing a mass murderous dictator because he was being out negotiated by his rival prior to his evil deeds.

The media would rather give the left in Washington and their supporter's credibility rather than report the truth. This must be what happened in Cuba, prior to the evil Castro and the other countries, worldwide that were taken over by the evil socialist/communist invaders. The media has said little to nothing when our economy and stock market was at all-time highs. Our unemployment was at all-time lows for Black Americans, Hispanic Americans and Asian Americans. The media has proven it could care less for the average Americans well-being! The far left socialists and media have one goal to remove President Trump even if it's at the expense of benefiting the American people.

Bulletin to our representatives in Congress! You

were voted to represent we the American people and be judged <u>solely</u> on how you have, through your legislation in Congress made our lives better! Lowest unemployment ever was very good not bad! Best economy ever was very good not bad! Stock market at an All-Time High was very good not bad! You should be judged <u>solely</u> on how the average Americans life has improved not how your wealth has improved. Listen-Pelosi, Schumer, Schiff and followers you're only successful when the average Americans are successful!! It's not about how much money you make it's about how the average Americans income and lives have improved!!

America do not fall for the media and far left con!! America's survival depends on all of us speaking out, refusing to give these far left socialist the ability to destroy what has made America the envy of the world!

Remember the biblical verse: "You shall know the truth and the truth will set you free."

Charles S. Togias: Author Political Correctness Is Total BS

AMERICAS DECEPTION MEDIA STYLE

(5/21/2020) — Published World Tribune (6/2/2020)

The title of my article is very appropriate for two reasons: It's the title of the first chapter of my book: **Political Correctness Is Total BS** and it is describing the main stream media at its worst. I was in the media as a sales representative and sales manager for many years after returning from serving in Vietnam and never witnessed the main stream media in such a compromising position. From 1971-1992 I was a sales representative and sales manager at an NBC affiliate in Syracuse, New York and was very proud to represent my station. That's when the main stream reported the news in an unbiased, professional manner and now it's become a total misrepresentation!

I am going to list 5 horrific examples that a school paper and their staff would report accurately if they had once ounce of character and credibility and compare it to our very self-serving and devious main stream media. These 5 topics have all been exposed to all Americans and are very concerning to anyone with principles and integrity. I am also going to compare how the main stream media have reacted to these events.

1. Biden's son getting millions of dollars as a consultant for a business he had no knowledge of and could not speak the language while Biden was Vice President. To make matters much worse Joe Biden pressured the Ukrainian government to fire their investigator who was assigned to look into this travesty. The media will tell you they covered the story. They did not see a big problem and eventually dropped it. It sounds good but is completely false and here is why. Here is my very simple question: What would have been the main stream media's reaction if Trump's son was involved in the exact same situation while Trump was in the White House? Do you think they would have ever dropped the story? It would be their major headline to this day and beyond!

2. Hillary was never charged for Russian collusion even though her foundation was giving over 100 million dollars by the Russians after they received 20% of our uranium. Remember by her own admission, on video, she proclaimed,

prior to this event, that she was dead broke. Please look up the video! The main stream media never proclaimed or supported claims that she was in Russia's pocket. They were too busy trying to frame Trump with these ridiculous accusations! Hillary got millions by the Russians and that's not collusion and Trump never received one penny from Russia and not one vote was ever changed during the 2016 election but that is collusion. The media and their allies want Trump out and will do or say anything to achieve their goal.

3. Judge Kavanagh was accused of rape, which has never been proven when he was in High School and the main stream went wild with glee. His accuser had no memory of any actual details just that in high he raped her. The democrats and their allies in the media were in a complete frenzy because they are convinced that the judge, if nominated to the Supreme Court would overturn Roe vs. Wade banding abortion rights and they and their supporters are 100% against that. Yet they say little to nothing regarding Biden's rape charges by a woman who can give specific details supporting her allegations and this was a few years ago.

That is what I call selective outrage or the big media con!

4. President Obama was of modest means when he entered the White House as President and now his worth is estimated to be somewhere between 50-100 million and the media has never investigated or mentioned it. Trump does not take a salary and the main stream media also never mentions it. Remember former President Harry Truman, a democrat, famous quote: "You can't get rich in Washington unless you're a crook." I am not accusing Obama of being a crook but I do know one thing. That if President Trump entered the White House with the exact same scenario as Obama did and Trump became a multi-millionaire he would be in jail. It would not matter if it was a crime or not to our fair minded media! They hate him and would make it look like a crime. They do not deliver the news they will distort the news if Trump is involved!

5. A hundred and fifty billion was given to Iran, the world's foremost sponsor of terrorism, by the Obama administration, at night and in cash as well as giving them the right to develop

nuclear weapons and the main stream media was not outraged. This is a complete disregard for humanity giving these Iranian savages, who are dedicated to destroying Israel and all those they are in conflict with and the media said little to nothing. The media did not consider Obama and his administration to be anti-sematic. They were too busy calling Trump anti sematic even thought his daughter married a Jew, converted to Judaism and is raising their daughter in the Jewish faith. The main stream media should hang its head in shame and anyone currently in the media, with an ounce of integrity should leave ASAP!

Our country with its Constitution and Judeo-Christian principles and values has been the beacon of the world. We are not perfect because humanity is not perfect, we are just better than any other country because we value all people regardless of color or religion. People from all over the world come to America and we should always be proud of our country. We should always question those, especially in our media that are now dedicated to lie and misrepresent themselves to achieve their misguided hateful agenda to destroy President Donald Trump! The main stream media has now become America's worst enemy because we have always relied on them for truth! As I have said previously the main stream media has gotten to where they now make the mafia look legitimate. The media is dedicated to deception for those who conflict with their agenda and no one conflicts more with their agenda than President Trump!! This hatred has made them compromise their principles and values!

I am ending with my personal quote:

"When the main stream media of any nation compromises truth to achieve their political, biased agenda by distorting the truth the nation is doomed for destruction"

Charles S. Togias: Author Political Correctness Is Total BS

JOE THE GENIUS BIDEN AND HIS SELECTIVE OUTRAGE

(5/28/2020)

When I see what Joe Biden says and does it makes me wonder if he thinks most Americans are stupid or he is so out of touch with reality that it makes sense to him. Either way America better wake up and realize what our future would be with him as President. Joe's latest comment regarding that Black Americans are not really black if they vote republican/President Trump is only one of many comments and assumptions he has tried to pass off as legitimate and normal?? I am going to discuss this latest idiotic statement as well as conclusions Biden is responsible for in this article and see if you feel as I do that a Biden presidency would be a bigger disaster to America and the world surpassing anything the corona visa pandemic inflicted. I may become redundant but I feel it must be fully examined to clarify who we are dealing with when contemplating a Biden Presidency!

All principle centered Americans should still be

outraged when Hunter Biden was hired as a consultant and paid huge amounts of money by the Ukraine and had no idea of the business he was consulting and could not even speak the language. Yet Biden, democrats and the main stream media, to this day have never seriously had to answer for their lack of concern. Then to compound this atrocity Joe Biden then had the Ukrainian prosecutor fired when he was going to look into this immoral travesty. If Biden had one ounce of principles and integrity he would have forced his son to give back all the money he received and been outraged. Instead he defended his son and the Ukrainian prosecutor was fired! This was beyond horrific and makes Biden and his son criminals by illegally pressuring and black mailing a foreign country. If any other American did this other than a politician we would be in jail. Remember America Joe Biden was Vice- President of the United States of America during this horrible criminal hiring situation!

Now Joe Biden calls black Americans which will not vote for him, not black. To enlighten you finger pointing Joe, the vast majority of black Americans are far from stupid. They want the opportunity to be self-sufficient and provide for themselves and their families. Success in business, school and sports build confidence, self-esteem and character. If Joe Biden was really interested in Black Americans as he proclaims he is, he should have been shouting from the roof tops when in just 3 short years the republicans under Trump registered the lowest black unemployment figures ever in America!! I as an American was thrilled and would have been just as thrilled if a democratic administration was responsible for the black Americans success. Of course that's because I don't have a selective agenda. Joe Biden has been in politics for the majority of his life and the political game for career politicians is smoke, mirrors and profit.

Joe would have been outraged if Trump's son was involved in the EXACT same situation as his son and that says everything about him and what we need to know about him and the media swamp rats that support him by remaining silent. Con-artists can come in all shapes and sizes but the way you distinguish them is through their selective outrage. They have 2 sets of standards, one for themselves and one for the rest of us!

Now if Black Americans voice their support for an administration whose efforts are helping them and their families become more successful people like self-serving Joe are outraged! All Americans better understand that politicians like Biden are not about helping us it's only about them!!! Especially with shifty Joe!!

My hope and prayer is that Black Americans will achieve continued success at the highest level and the self-serving politicians who are only interested in themselves can go to hell!!

Charles S. Togias: Author Political Correctness Is Total BS. Create Loyal Customers in an Unloyal World

ALL LIVES MATTER

(6/13/2020)

What happened to George Floyd was a complete injustice and cannot be explained away by anyone that is principle centered. To kneel on his throat for 9 minutes while he is saying that he cannot breathe is murder. It should be investigated and due punishment should and will be forthcoming. George Floyd was a career criminal but did not deserve this type of justice handed out by police because **All lives matter.**

The riots and destruction that followed is also criminal behavior and all those involved should be prosecuted and brought to justice. The burning down of buildings, robbing of stores, the murdering and rocks thrown at police that had nothing to do with the Floyd matter should be also prosecuted to the full extent of the law. Those committing these crimes and their anarchist backers should be identified and thrown in jail because **All lives matter.**

These anarchists that commit or support those that commit these atrocities always seem to be able to justify their blatant criminal activity while always pointing their finger at all those they opposed. They have a selective sense of justice. Some black leaders like Al Sharpton and Jesse Jackson are rarely outraged when those in their community commit horrific crimes against non-blacks outside their community. They will always call America a racist country when a black man is unjustifiably harmed but are never concerned when the opposite is done. They don't understand that their selective outrage makes them complete hypocrites and phonies because **All lives matter.**

The definition of a racist is opposing anyone for the sole reason of the color of their skin and I believe those that do this are stupid morons and thank heaven are not this nations vast majority. The vast majority of Americans are good God-loving people. I might be naïve but I believe most Americans and people, in general, do not discriminate against color. As I referenced in the Racist chapter of my book: **Political Correctness Is Total BS.** I said most people discriminate against behavior not color. I have many great friends that are black and great people. They are kind and considerate and never go out of their way to find fault or cause hardship. Because of their solid upbringing they understand that **All lives matter.**

Don't be fooled America these so called demonstrations on behalf of Mr. Floyd's death with the burning of buildings, looting and killing of officers not involved in the in George Floyd death should be condemned by all Americans. It is a complete con and gives these far left anarchists an excuse and reason to revolt against America and our scared principles of life and liberty for all. These far left anarchist have no belief in God and want to destroy our Constitution. Our religious beliefs and Constitution are what made America the envy of the world. They could care less about justice they only care about their far left anti God doctrine. Their goal is to destroy America!

These far left haters will only gain credibility when they understand that **All lives matter.**

Charles S. Togias: Author Political Correctness Is Total BS

CHARLES S. TOGIAS

FAR LEFTS CONTINUAL POLITICAL OUTRAGE IS THEIR VERSION OF SMOKE AND MIRRORS

(6/15/2020)

Politicians that are always pointing at their rivals while their districts are in shambles must be practical jokers and think of us non politicians as stupid and gullible. Americans are currently witnessing now how many of our self-righteous far left politicians are either condoning these radical far left demonstrations against police or speaking out with rage and vengeance against **all police**. Wanting to defund the police or eliminating them in many districts altogether. When I see this on a continual basis all I can say is: are you frigging kidding me? Far left politicians accusing all police of taking advantage of their authority is the equivalent of Dracula accusing the Red Cross of not using proper procedures when taking blood.

Many of these far left finger pointing politicians, who have served in Congress for many years, have become multi-millionaires while many of their districts are in shambles. The unfortunate people residing in their districts live in complete poverty. These hypocrites and political finger pointers are well beyond self-righteous they are, I believe criminals. Politicians were put in office for one reason to "serve we the people" not their own best interests. I continue in my articles to use former President Harry Truman's quote: "you cannot get rich in Washington unless you're a crook."

I don't have a problem with any politicians becoming successful, even financially in Washington but only if their districts and those they serve benefit greatly. If their districts are in shambles and their constituents are not benefiting from their decisions and policies they should never benefit, especially financially. They should never, ever become wealthy if their districts are not thriving! All Americans better understand: When politicians become very wealthy when their districts are suffering you can be guaranteed they have a big credibility issue.

In my book: Political Correctness Is Total BS I strongly urge that all 535 politicians now serving in Washington, in the House and Senate should have a complete review of their entire net worth prior to taking office and what it is currently. Those that have not gained great wealth as a result of their serving should be singled out and given great recognition. They are truly people of great integrity. Those, on the other hand, that have become very wealthy should also be recognized. Also if their districts are in shambles and they have become millionaires there should be a way for them to have to pay retribution to the needy in their districts! I can 100% guarantee, if this was ever proposed on the House or Senate floor it would be defeated immediately. The Washington hustlers will never approve anything that takes away from their power and money. It would be similar to voting for term limit!

P.T. Barnum said "There is a sucker born every minute." America we have been suckers long enough. We must be united and hold those that we elect in Washington accountable for their actions and confront and examine their perceived outrage as well as income. Let's stop being taken for suckers!! Remind our politicians that many of us may have been born at night but not last night!

Charles S. Togias: Author Political Correctness Is Total BS

JOURNALISM'S FAR LEFT RADICAL AGENDA WILL LEAD TO AMERICAS DESTRUCTION

(6/20/2020)

Webster's Dictionary's definition of journalism is: the collection and editing of news through the media (b) the public press (c) an academic study concerned with the collection and editing of news or management of a news medium. Unfortunately it does not include the word truth as an over-riding prerequisite because I guess that must be in the eyes of the beholder. Without truth journalists must feel they have a right to distort.

As a result the main stream media must have concluded that their version and spin of the news is their right as "journalists." Their political prejudice allows them to deliver their spin to help those they are aligned with and benefit from. I am sure this is exactly what happened in Germany prior to Hitler and in Cuba prior to Castro. Distorting the news to benefit an agenda that will only result in self-serving gratification while destroying their opposition!

In 1933 Hitler appointed Hermann Goring Minister of the Interior. His job was to **defund police departments** so they would not interfere with his Brown shirts whose job it was to riot, burn, beat up and kill those citizens in opposition to his evil efforts to assure his election. Does this sound familiar with our Journalist? Far left media bias will only result in the destruction of America!

The far left billionaires with the support of their trained political and media counter-parts are dedicated to changing everything that has made America great to serve their own best interests. Our Constitution and Judeo-Christian principles and values has been the rock upon which made our government and country the envy of the world. The far left haters want to change America and our main stream media is unfortunately bought and paid for and is in "lock step" with these far left America haters. When the main stream media is told to jump their only response is how high!

The mainstream media and far-left politicians are America's biggest problem because they have sold their souls to tranny to benefit themselves! They do not report the news they purposely distort the news to benefit those they report to. They are America's biggest enemies and will be our destruction if not confronted and overthrown!

To support a far left government agenda is the equivalent of supporting Hitler, Stalin and Castro three of the most evil humans ever created. The far left billionaires with their political and media puppets are dedicated to causing destruction to America and our scared principles of truth and justice for all. We must never allow them to continue to achieve their evil doctrine. Our children and grand-children's lives and liberty are at stake.

When we see these riots of burning, looting, rocks thrown at police and innocent people being beat up in the name of George Floyd, being justified as righteous anger it only goes to prove my point that the media will distort the truth to meet an agenda. Their agenda is to cause chaos among Americans by **demanding the defunding of police departments**. This is the way the far left justify revolution!

Let's see how the crooked media responds to the Oklahoma Trump rally. They will be outraged and claim it will result in tens of thousands of people contracting the coronavirus. Citing many will die and Trump should be impeached for allowing the rally. It is total hypocrisy!

This is the same media that has said nothing about the tens of thousands of demonstrators nationwide that were involved in the George Floyd funeral and demonstrations. In the past they also said little to nothing about crooked Hillary's emails and her great overnight wealth at the hands of the Russian uranium deal. They over looked and dismissed Joe Biden's son making millions as a consultant for a business he knew nothing about and could not speak the language. The media still remained silent when Genius Joe had the Ukrainian prosecutor fired who was looking into this travesty!

Winston Churchill once said: "Some people's idea of free speech is that they are free to say what they like, but if anyone says anything back that is outrage."

Charles S. Togias: Author Political Correctness Is Total BS

TODAY'S POLITICAL UNDERWORLD AND ITS FOCUS TO DESTROY AMERICA

(7/1/2020)

My book: **Political Correctness Is Total BS**, which is the 4th edition, cannot be more relevant than right now. I exposed the secular left for wanting to destroy our basic principles: our Judeo-Christian values and Constitution, which if they succeed will destroy America! These far left anarchists billionaires, politicians and their paid flunkies are trying to destroy America and everything that made us the envy of the world. I am going to emphasize to them and the world that all of God's Children's Lives Matter! All LIVES MATTER regardless of color! To qualify a life in any other way is in itself prejudice!

My heart goes out to the Black communities because after, Martin Luther King, who was a great leader and tremendous asset to all of America, was assassinated, the black community had to endure leaders like Al Sharpton and Jesse Jackson. Both are political finger pointers never having a plan on how to improve black lives. They only point fingers at others and never lead by example. To emphasize this can you name a black community that has benefited by them or any of their democratic political representatives that have served in these communities? Great leaders improve the skills and behavior of those they lead. Horrible leaders only point fingers and blame others. President Ronald Regan said: "The only experience you gain in politics is how to be political"

To this day I have always hoped and prayed that Thomas Sowell, a great black American with tremendous literary experience would have been the black communities and Americas inspiration to help improve all of Americans future. Mr. Sowell was born in North Carolina and raised in Harlem by his aunt. He attended Harvard where he was Valedictorian of his class. He has written many books including one of my all-time favorites: Black Rednecks/ White Liberals. Mr. Sowell always stated that education does not start in school it starts in the home. I wanted, so much for him to run for President!

The functional family is humanity's greatest asset because it stresses love, discipline, responsibility and encourages and rewards success. Great families will never condone bad behavior to be the means to an end. Personal responsibility means doing the right thing at the right time! Great leaders reward good behavior understanding that you can never gain acceptance with violence toward others while horrible, misguided leaders will always give a reason to do so!

The Black Lives Matter demonstrations are an excuse to riot, steal, attack police and cause total disruption to all of America to achieve a self-serving agenda designed to over-throw and change America! Now they want to destroy all of our symbols including Abraham Lincoln statues and Mount Rushmore. Do not be fooled America those paying for this destruction hate America and everything we have stood for. Can you imagine what this world would be like with them in charge? Evil is what evil does!!

The left talks about the intolerance of America. They should trying doing this disruption in China, Russia, Cuba and North Korea. If they did they would be able to understand why America is the world's greatest country.

Charles S. Togias: Author Political Correctness Is Total BS

THE SQUAD OF WASHINGTON, DC AND THE CONTINUAL CON OF AMERICA

Published World Tribune (7/19/2020)

When we continually hear the outrage of the four Democratic members of 'The Squad' in Washington DC against America and our history I am in complete disbelieve. Congresswomen Ilhan Omar from Minnesota, Rashida Tlaib from Michigan (both Muslim), Ayanna Pessary Massachusetts and of course the former bartender now political authority Alexandria Ocasio Cortez from New York have now become the Democratic party and America's voice condemning our history and practices involving America's supposedly inhumanity to our citizens. All of them want to change America into a socialist country and many Americans are finding them credible and it's astonishing to me!

I am going to focus briefly on their history/past and see if they have an ounce of credibility.

1. Ilhan Omar is Muslim, Somali-American, Minnesota Congresswoman and migrated to America at age 17. She is very critical of Israel's treatment of Palestine and thinks America is very unfair and must become socialist.

2. Rashida Tlaib is Muslim, Palestinian-American, Michigan Congresswomen and when elected was quoted as saying "We are going to go there to impeach the Mother F....er" (President Trump). In other words a real classy lady!! She also supports: boycotts, divestments, and sanctions against Israel!!

3. Ayanna Pressley Congresswomen from Massachusetts. She has now been considered radical because of her association with this group.

4. Alexandria Ocasio Cortez was a bartender with no political experience. Does not have any personal or business accomplishments but she considers herself an authority on America and our history. She is a non-achieving socialist dedicated to changing America into a socialist country. A.O.C. trying to pass herself as an authority on anything, other than mixing drinks,

should be a complete embarrassment to the entire nation as well as herself.

These four misguided individuals have become the voice of the Democratic Party.

As I previously referenced two of 'The Squad' are Muslim and I only want to reference this because they should, above all others in Washington understand what real oppression is. I wrote in my book: **Political Correctness Is Total BS** 5TH Chapter entitled **Terrorism** the following:

Here are two examples I found when researching Sharia Law: Let's compare the Muslim Fundamentalists religion to the religious right in our country and see if there is a comparison.

Afghanistan: Strict interpretation of Islamic law calls for the death penalty for any women found in the company of a man other than a close family member. Sexual activity is assumed to have happened. A women Jamila, was found guilty of trying to leave the country with such a man. She was caught and stoned to death on March 28, 1996.

The second example is again Afghanistan: Under the previous Taliban regime, a woman, Nurbibi, 40 and a man Turylai, 38, were stoned to death in a public assembly using palm size stones. They were found guilty of non-martial sex. Turylia was dead within 10 minutes, but Nurbibi had to be finished off by dropping a large stone on her head.

Mr. Wali, head of the Office for the Propagation of Virtue and the Prohibition of Vice, expressed satisfaction with the execution. "I am very happy because it means that the rule of Islam is being implemented." These executions as well as hand amputations for convicted thieves are regarded as religious occasions and are not viewed by non-Muslims (End of book reference).

This is in addition to allowing honor killings of a Muslim woman if she dates a non- Muslim man. Those committing these savage crimes against women cannot be prosecuted for this, as it is justified in their religion. Also their women are completely covered from head to toe in compliance with their faith. America is not perfect but there has never been any American government, in our history that would condone this treachery against women. It would be impossible for anyone that is seeking the truth to compare or condemn America for its past and our Judeo-Christian values with these horrific religious practices.

Coming from what most normal human beings would consider a demonic culture such as mentioned above and continually finding fault with America means you are either in complete denial of your Fundamentalist past or trying to be very deceptive. America has never been this horrific to women of any persuasion. To condone the burning down of American businesses, stoning police and stealing in the name of Black Lives Matter or any group to justify your perceived righteous anger against America and its past is a complete con job.

Now the far left secular anarchists want to tear down statues of American hero's such as Presidents Washington, Jefferson, and Lincoln just to name a few for their perceived atrocities against America! Their goal is to destroy the greatest country in the world by falsifying its past under the pretext of their outrage for treatment of black Americans.

We have researched and found that Black Lives Matter is a global hate group funded by anarchists billionaire socialist's haters of America, our Constitution and our Judeo-Christian principles and values. All of which has made America the envy of the world. Yet many of the far left in Congress and the media are either falling for the con or being well paid to go lock step in the disruption. 'The Squad' has become a voice of that group.

Now these radical democrats all over America are

calling for the defunding of police departments. Be aware of what Hitler did in 1933 when he defunded the police departments so the Brown shirts could destroy Germany! Hitler gained power through these tactics and the outcome was devastating to the world. If you want to live in another Hitler like Germany go along with the con!

God Bless America!! The greatest country ever created!!!

Charles S. Togias: Author Political Correctness Is Total BS

SECULAR ANARCHISTS AT WAR WITH AMERICA

(7/19/2020)

Black Lives Matter is a worldwide funded terrorist's organization and is in itself racists. A member/follower of this terrorist group recently shot and killed a woman for saying that All Lives Matter. Any group that does not recognize and value the lives of all of humanity and only cares about the lives of one ethnic group is racists. If you don't value the lives all people of color whether they are yellow, brown, red, white etc. you are a racists! Period!

BLM have supplied bricks at demonstration sites as well as baseball bats to those that support their cause. Since there was no construction at these sites and no ball parks why do you think these items were there and who put them there? These are criminals and they will violate anyone of any color who disagrees with their socialist, communist anti God philosophy. These far left animals should be identified and prosecuted to the full extent of the law regardless of color. Giving them a pass because they perform these atrocities like looting, burning of stores, stoning police and attacking anyone with another point of view under the title of Black Lives Matter is beyond ridiculous. They are criminals pure and simple!

BLM is funded by secular billionaires and they are dedicated to destroying America. They hate that America was built on our faith in God and want to eliminate our Constitution. Those in the main stream media and their political followers in Washington are bought and paid for because they will never confront this treachery. They have sacrificed their souls as well as their principles, if they ever had them, for power, money and acceptance. To prove this you can now be arrested for attending your place of wordship but can gather by the thousands and violently demonstrate without suffering any consequences. I thought there is separation of church and state? The main stream media and the political flunkies are in lock step with this con game and remain silent!

Remember America we have been instructed by God to Love thy neighbor and to do unto others as you would have them do unto you! In fact the whole New Testament talks about love and kindness for all! Yet the far left hate and criticize America's heritage and our belief in God.

Compare this philosophy with the BLM, the main

stream media and their far left supporter's perceived righteous anger in light of the Floyd killing. George Floyd was a very bad man and career criminal but never should have died in the way he did. It was murder. I am also sure that many black officers have killed white criminals that also may be questionable. I will never justify the murder of anyone. I also understand that career criminals violate and murder many innocence people and most times will resist arrest. Let's also understand that Police have a very difficult job with tremendous pressure.

In my book: **Political Correctness Is Total BS** 14th Chapter entitled: **Police Abused** I stated the following. There is an old saying that the definition of a conservative is a liberal who has been mugged. When you face a life and death situation, you have a completely different thought process. Survival is a wonderful reality check.

It is so easy to condemn those you oppose but if you do you must do so with credibility. BLM opposes America, our values, God and our Constitution and does so with violence and hatred. Their hateful message of looting, burning and killing those they oppose exposes who they are! They will never be able to give an example of a country that compares with us!

BLM main goal is to destroy America and everything we stand for. They are a criminal organization that hates America and our history and that is why they want to destroy the statues of our presidents such as: Washington, Jefferson and even the great emancipator Abraham Lincoln. They are trying to destroy our churches and even statues of Jesus Christ. They must be exposed as to who they are and be confronted with as much righteous anger as needed.

America is not perfect because humanity is not perfect we are just the best country ever and that's why people come from all over the world to live here. Life, liberty and the pursuit of happiness is what America offers. Socialism and communism are countries people flee from. To prove this how many people have we seen crossing shark infested waters going from Florida to Cuba!

America please do not be conned by the secular anarchists haters of our society they have an anti-God America hating agenda! The problem we must identify and confront is the new far left Democratic Party is in lock step with this anti America agenda.

God Bless America!

Charles S. Togias: Author Political Correctness Is Total BS

AMERICAS ENEMIES FROM WITHIN

(8/4/2020)

Today we Americans are eye witnesses to a revolution within our own borders that, if not confronted will change America forever! This calculated strategy has been well thought out for many years by those that want to destroy America and has been implemented one step at a time and very carefully planned. It is like water on stone you are not aware of its impact until it's too late to change their manipulated outcome.

It started many years ago when prayer and our pledge of alliance was removed from the class room. This was done claiming that it was discriminatory to those that do not believe in God as well as those that were not committed to our American values. These are the same anti-God hypocrites that said kneeling in protest for our National Anthem is fine and in fact were encouraged by the NFL because it demonstrates your first amendment rights. This is the same NFL that criticized then prohibited Christian quarterback Tim Tebow for kneeling in Prayer some years ago. I guess kneeling in prayer is horrible but disrespecting our flag and those who died for it is acceptable to the NFL and professional sports. Those that govern them and find this acceptable are despicable and have sold their souls!!

These far left anti-God anarchists are determined to change America from a God loving democratic republic to a socialist, communist secular country void of our scared traditional values. They have continued their conspiracy by encouraging the tearing down of our forefather's statues, including Jesus Christ, defacing churches and any and all of our historical past. They hate our belief in God and know that if they can remove God from America they will succeed in their treachery. By the way I thought there was separation between Church and State in America yet we were ordered not to attend church or any place of worship because of the Corona pandemic and your close proximity to others and could be arrested but you could demonstrate by the thousands in the streets without fear of retribution!! Maybe we should classify that as a double anti-God hypocrisy standard! Typical far left BS.

Black Lives Matter is funded by these atheists and has become a huge part of this conspiracy. If Black Lives really mattered to the BLM group they would put millions upon millions of dollars into finding a solution to the tremendous criminal problems plaguing the black community. They should institute 24 hour counseling from respected corporate and civic leaders such as: Thomas Sowell, Larry Elder and my new common sense friend Leo Terrell to name a few. There are many very successful black business executives that could shine a helpful light to those in the black community. Instead of pointing at the problem fix it. My personal evaluation of leadership is: "Great leaders improve the skills and behavior of those they lead." On the other hand horrible leaders are always pointing at everyone else and never fix anything! Can you hear me Al Sharpton?

Example: Now instead of fixing the problem many in Congress have referred to these riots in Seattle, Portland, Chicago, Minneapolis, New York and other cities as peaceful demonstration even though buildings are burned and looted, while police and innocent people are shot and killed including infants. These rioters are armed with rocks and bats many supplied to them prior to them arriving at the scene. Those in Congress that claim it's a peaceful demonstration never have to answer why these items were there before the riot took place!

Even after these facts are known Congress was

still in denial. When listening to the William Barr, U.S. Attorney General Interrogation and some of Congresses outrage when questioning Mr. Barr I could not listen long as it was idiotic to say the least. Congressional Representatives David Cicilline RI, Lou Correa CA, James Raskin MD and Jayapal Pramila WA all democrats still claim that these riots are nothing but peaceful demonstrations and are becoming violent because of federal troops sent there by President Trump.

There is an old saying: That there are three types of people you cannot negotiate with: Crazy people, Stupid people and Irrational people and after hearing these out cries in Congress regarding these so called demonstrations and them being classified as "peaceful demonstrations" I understand why.

Now these far left geniuses in the House and Senate want to defund police and remove all guns from all Americans. They really believe it will make our country much safer??? Chicago has a ban on all guns how is it working there? They have the highest murder rate in the country and rank as one of the highest in the world! Do these geniuses really feel that criminals will turn in their guns? It's like ordering a mechanic to turn in his tool box! If he does how does he make a living? If they really feel criminals will turn in their guns they are crazy, stupid and irrational and should not be allowed outdoors without adult supervision.

All of this makes me have real questions and concerns regarding the corona worldwide pandemic and its timing and origins. Did it just happen and infect the whole world by the tens of millions or was it a calculated devious plan to destroy mankind as we know it and who will benefit? If so this is Stalin and Hitler type treachery that is beyond horrific. Who is orchestrating this and how can we defeat this diabolical revolution?

Patrick Henry quote: "Is life so dear, or peace so sweet, as to be purchased at the price of chains and slavery? Forbid it Almighty God. I know not what course others may take but as for me, give me liberty or give me death"

I pray for life, liberty and the pursuit of happiness for **ALL** Americans-forever!!

Stay strong and God Bless America!!

Charles S. Togias: Author Political Correctness Is Total BS

DEMOCRATIC MARXISTS LEADERS BEYOND HYPOCRITICAL

(8/16/2020)

Featured World Tribune (8/17/2020)

Remember very recently when a St. Louis couple Mr. and Mrs. McCloskey was confronted by an angry mob that broke into their community? Mr. McCloskey is a lawyer and a strong advocate of civil rights for all. The couple armed with weapons confronted the mob. They were defending their lives, liberty and property. The couple was very frightened because of the mass destructions of burning, looting and attacking of civilians and police happening all over our country. Their community is gated and many of those entering the community were thugs dedicated to causing violence and harm to those they encountered. Most of these so called rioters that we have witnessed nightly on the news are dedicated to destroying these cities because they are criminal anarchists and our supported financially by far left anarchists and major corporations with an anti-

American agenda. These are not demonstrations by God loving people of our country trying to right wrongs; they are sponsored by anti-God American haters. Just imagine what America would become with them in charge.

Yet law makers like Nancy Pelosi, Chuck Schumer and their far left Democratic counter parts in these devastated cities agreed with the couple's arrest. Moreover they have classified these riots as peaceful. Leaders of these Democratic run cities like New York, Chicago, Portland, Seattle, and many others, that are in complete chaos blame President Trump for these atrocious and deteriorating conditions . These political hacks are professional do nothing finger pointing hypocrites that are not qualified to lead yet they are always pointing their finger at others. They take no responsibility for anything negative that happens under their watch. They just blame others!

Nancy Pelosi and many others serving in Congress who have armed security and live in gated communities are complete hypocrites for their perceived outrage with the McCloskey's. They will only gain an ounce of credibility with me, if they tear down their own walls and completely disarm their own security services. These Washington hypocrites only care about themselves. Many of them especially on the left lie, cheat and criticize opponents while never taking responsibility themselves. We the people that they supposedly serve are jeopardized with these riots while they are pointing fingers at their opposition. Please America do not be fooled they do not care about you, your family or your safety! If they cared about you these riots would be over the day they started. How long do you think they would have lasted in the neighborhood of a member of Congress?

I want to end this article with a very simple solution to end these riots! Israel has a spray that is guaranteed to disperse these rioters without causing physical harm. It has a very strong sunk like smell and is very effective at dispersing a large crowd. They use it at their borders with great effectiveness. Developed by Israel researchers, the spray can be swallowed and not cause injury or harm. It would be a very simple way to bring peace and law and order to these crime ridden cities.

My question to our self-righteous "leaders" in Washington, especially on the left: If I know about this spray shouldn't they know about the spray and if they do, why aren't they using it? Could the answer be they want these riots to continue to help their political agenda? It not does matter how many innocence police or civilians are killed or injured as long as they achieve their self-serving agenda. Are they rooting for chaos?

America is the greatest country in the world and I pray we will be able to overcome this manipulative deception and hypocrisy! Remember todays far left version of common sense is meant to deceive!

Charles S. Togias: Author Political Correctness Is Total BS

POLITICAL SELLING OF SOULS... MONEY IS THE ROOT OF THEIR EVIL

(9/7/2020)

Robert Kennedy Jr. recently said "People in authority lie." I am going to expand on that and say especially politicians. When I hear these far left politicians bought and paid for by the billionaire America haters distorting the truth to fit their political agenda I am in disbelief. Recently Joe Biden was in a news conference telling America how horrible President Trump is and how he is destroying America. How the President has cheated America for his own best interest and only looks to personally profit from his Presidency. Joe Biden saying these things to the American people is the equivalent of Dracula accusing the Red Cross of having inhumane methods when taking blood.

When Mr. Biden is criticizing anyone for cheating, collusion and being under handed I am in utter disbelief. Let's look at his and his parties' less than honorable history. Mr. Biden has been in Washington almost 50 years and has personally profited greatly for his service. He is a multi-millionaire for his service to "we the people" even though he has been a Washington failure. His "honorable" son Hunter Biden was paid millions by the Ukraine for a consulting job he knew nothing about and could not even speak the language! When the Ukraine hired someone to look into this situation Joe Biden used his influence to have the inspector fired which he admitted on Television. Can you possibly imagine what the main stream media would report if it was Trump and his son who were involved? Joe Biden criticizing Mr. Trump or any other politicians for any political misdeeds is beyond horrific! It's total hypocrisy at its lowest level and he should never be believed by anyone with an IQ over 50. Biden over his political years should have lost all credibility instead he is his party and the main stream medias hero.

In fact let's look at other Democratic politicians and determine if they have the ability to point fingers at their rivals. Hillary Clinton was on television some years ago claiming she was dead broke. So benevolent Hillary started the Clinton Foundation to help those in need and within a very short period of time became a multi-millionaire. Hillary's estimated worth is now over $100 million. While her foundation gave around 3-4% to those in need. By the way when she assisted Russia with their uranium efforts Russia put over $100,000,000 in the Clinton Foundation but that was never considered collusion by the selective Democratic condemners or their partners in the media!

Barack Obama who was not a millionaire before becoming President now has an estimated worth of between $70-100 million. I am sure there are many, many more elected politicians on both sides who have accumulated great wealth while serving in Congress. They are in the pocket of special interest groups and have sold "we the people" out yet they are always trying to accuse their rivals of wrong doing.

Now the liberal Democrats in Washington want to defund police all over America because of the criminal conduct of a few police officers. The vast majority of police in America have saved tens of thousands of lives annually yet the far left lump all police as bad. How many lives were saved by the police in New York during 9/11? How many American citizens are protected by police when criminals are attacking them? Yet the far left have declared that all police are bad and in doing so risk the safety of the average American. Their answer is to defund all police departments nationwide.

I have a better idea. I propose instead of defunding police we defund all politicians' salaries whose districts are in shambles. My proposal is to judge each congressional district on its current status and evaluate whether the community has benefited from their elected representative. Are these districts crime rates going down? Are robbery's and murders decreasing in their districts? If not put the blame where it belongs on those righteous Washington representatives that have been elected to help bring peace and prosperity to the districts they serve. If they have failed each year there should be a 12.5 % refund of the representatives pay that would go directly into helping the citizens of that community. If the congressional representative served two terms, eight years and their district never improves they would be paid 0 if elected to a third term. This could also serve as a way to enforce term limits without having a vote by Congress! Also there must be strict unbiased inspectors monitoring each representative and the outside contributions by special interest groups while they are serving!

Unfortunately the Presidential election of 2020 will be the most important in our history and if the far left Democrats win America, as we know it, may never recover. Riots in our streets justified by the left and positioned by them as peaceful protests are destroying America! When I heard that the mayor of Portland, Oregon Ted Wheeler has blamed President Trump and not himself and Black Lives Matter for the horrible killing of police and citizens and the looting and burning of businesses in his community I knew instantly that he along with his party are for these atrocities. They feel if they will not condemn these horrible events, it will help them politically and I knew instantly that they have sold their souls for power and money! If Mayor Ted's job is not to protect the citizens who elected him what is his job? Ted's finger pointing outrage was despicable to say the least!

Black Lives Matter is a criminal, far left organization and must never be characterized as anything other. I as well as most law abiding Americans are always in favor of peaceful demonstrations that help those in need. Peaceful organizations never start fires and loot buildings and attack those that peacefully disagree with them. Only terrorist's organization do. We must never forget that bricks were supplied at many of these demonstration sites days before the demonstrations started. This organization is a far left anti American group dedicated to destroying the America that we know.

Martin Luther King was one of America's greatest leaders and he would be horrified if he saw what the BLM group was doing to our country. I was and still am a great admirer of Dr. King because he was a very righteous man with great integrity. Dr. King would never condone the destruction of businesses, violating innocent people, police and neighborhoods under the pretext of helping them achieve equality. Peaceful protest is a God giving right in America and I will always defend the right of each citizen to participate and voice their concerns. Anarchy on the other hand is evil and has no place in America!

To continue their diabolical rage the radical left in America has resorted to the tearing down of statues of our great leaders past and present, defacing places of worship and symbols of Jesus Christ, and attacking and minimizing our Constitution. These horrific anti American acts are all a far left plot to change America into a socialist/communist, country. Americas far left haters are Anarchists supported and paid for by billionaires and their mission is to destroy the greatest country in the world and many Democratic politicians have joined the revolution. If they gain power in November do not be surprised if they tear down the Statue of Liberty and Mount Rushmore!!

I want to end my article with a positive message by revealing that many Black Americans, who I respect, are backing President Trump and the Republican Party. Very principle centered people like: Civil rights attorney Leo Terrell, hall of fame football player Hershel Walker, Larry Elder, Kimberly Klacik, Horace Cooper, Bob Woodson and many more. All of these great Americans I have tremendous respect for because they will not compromise their principles and integrity for blind loyalty! In fact it's estimated that President Trump will receive two and a half times more black votes than he received in 2016! Many of our black brothers and sisters are not falling for the far left con because they know America is not perfect we are just better than anywhere else!

We must never compromise our values because socialists/communists countries are the countries everyone is fleeing from because they are horrible places to live!!

Be strong America and never compromise truth!! God Bless America!!

Charles S. Togias: Author Political Correctness Is Total BS

CHARLES S. TOGIAS

MARKETING OF A NAME VERSUS THE DOCTRINE... (SMOKE AND MIRRORS)

(9/21/2020)

There is no God loving American that can argue, dispute or criticize the phrase Black Lives Matter. Black lives and in fact all lives regardless of race, color and creed matter! Those that named their organization Black Lives Matter were marketing geniuses because how can anyone argue with that name? The problem is it's not the name it is their doctrine that is very alarming! BLM is a terrorist organization and I believe this because they are dedicated to destroying America and our faith and principles. If the Nazis where smart enough before World War Two and had similar marketing expertise and referred to themselves as All Lives Matter they may still be causing worldwide riots, death and destruction under a false narrative! Remember actions speak much louder than words and BLM's actions were horrific during these riots!

If you do not believe in God and do not have a

love for humanity anything goes. We need to know and identify the leaders of BLM and expose their committed doctrine! Are they God Loving people that want all people safe and stress worldwide love and unity or are they a terrorist organization dedicated to over throwing our democratic republic? It should be very easy to research their founder's doctrine and beliefs.

When we all witnessed the horrible riots orchestrated by BLM in many American cities over the unfortunate deaths of black criminals by some police most Americans were horrified. While many of our bought and paid for politicians said these horrible riots were peaceful. No one with an ounce of integrity can condone murder! Only bought and paid for politicians with a self-serving agenda can!

I have real concerns with organizations like BLM and their ill-advised donors as well as anarchists, far left billionaires who own the main stream media and many politicians and their motives regarding America and our heritage. I believe the radical left want to remove God and our sacred traditions as well as our Constitution and change our democracy to a socialist, Godless country. I have found that many people will sell their souls for money! Something I and the vast majority of Americans cannot do in good conscience!!

These anarchists want to defund police and remove the Second Amendment, eliminating Americans the right to bear arms. Similar to what Hitler did in 1933 with the brown shirts to gain control of Germany. The rest is history. So I ask how can this possibly make Americans safe? The only thing it will do is make Americans vulnerable and unable to protect themselves from criminals and the government. Remember criminals will never give up their weapons as it is their way of profiting from their evil deeds. Only law abiding citizens will be in danger! Of course politicians will continue to have armed security so they don't care.

Remember America Godless people have no one to answer to but themselves and their evil doctrine. If America removes God and our Constitution from America as well as defund police and remove Americans right to bear arms we will never recover and I believe that is the far left political socialist's intention. America is the envy of the world because of our Judeo- Christian faith and our Constitution! We must never allow any group especially those seculars with a far left anti American agenda to change the greatest country in the world. America is not perfect we are just better than any other country in the world and my hope is we will continually improve by focusing on what made America Great! Faith, truth and principles!

I want to end my article by saying I was not a fan of candidate Donald Trump until I heard that the Washington insiders and the main stream media hated him. It was a hated I had never seen before. When I found this out I said I better take another look. Then I saw that Black, Hispanic and Asian Americans unemployment was at an all-time low. The stock market was also at an all-time high as was the average Americans income so I knew then he was not the typical good talking do nothing politician that we have all become use to he was a doer!! Many Washington politicians become multi-millionaires while their districts are in shambles! They are great do nothing self-serving finger pointers. President Trump improves the lives of those he serves! All Americans should judge all politicians on results not their BS!

God Bless America Our Constitution and Judeo-Christian values!!

Charles S. Togias: Author Political Correctness Is Total BS

SMOKE AND MIRRORS BIDEN STYLE...

(11/1/2020)

I continually hear how outraged Joe Biden is regarding what he refers to as President Trump's continued lies and misrepresentations. Joe has stated many times how Donald Trump never tells the truth and is a complete con-artist. When I hear this from Joe I try to determine if he is serious or just trying to amuse his audience. I don't want to refer to Joe as a typical politician because, his now revealed deception in his past, says that he is much worse. A con artist and thief has no room or right to preach to others.

Joe along with his son Hunter have been involved with taking money and hugely profiting in their dealings with Russia, China and the Ukraine and who knows who else while he was Vice President of the United States. This was confirmed by Tony Bobulinski who worked very closely with the Biden's in these, what now can be referred to as elicited ventures. Hunter Biden, who had no experience in almost anything, became a multi-millionaire with these interactions as well as Joe and his brother profiting greatly. Joe has spent 47 years in Washington and his net worth is estimated at over $30 million. The main stream media has lost whatever credibility they had by not even exposing or questioning him on these very suspicious and criminal transactions. When Joe says he works for we the people do not believe it! It's a complete con!!

Can you even imagine what the media would do if Trump's son was involved in these exact situations while Trump was in office? Anyone that thinks the media would react no differently is beyond biased and in complete denial of the truth! The main stream media is now a far left group that is becoming very secular and socialist. Their hatred for our President is very disturbing and beyond anything I could have ever imagined. I very strongly believe those that now own the media are far left billionaires who want to remove our Constitution and our Judeo-Christian values. If these socialist, anarchist and communist get their way America and our scared values will be completely destroyed.

For example if Biden gets elected and the House and Senate go democrat I can guarantee that they will pack the Supreme Court, eliminate fossil fuel, create open borders, eliminate filibustering and the Electoral College just to name a few. Abortion which I consider America's modern day holocaust will continue to kill babies in and out of the womb. If this is allowed to happen the America that was once the envy of the world will be destroyed.

The far left democratic party are anti-God and have told Americans that if they attended church they can be arrested because of the pandemic and their close interaction with those that attend but if they demonstrate in the streets by the thousands they will not be in violation of our laws. I always thought that there was separation between church and state. These far left predators are very dangerous and want to change America into a secular anti God country. When they die they will rot in hell for eternity but until then will cause great hardship for those of us they violate!

Remember China that created this virus is a communist country and the secular far left billionaires, politicians together with these socialists are all involved in this conspiracy. I for one will never give in to this demonic attack on our great principles and Judeo-Christian values!

I will never sacrifice my principles for power and money because my faith in God is everything to me!

"All tyranny needs to gain a foothold is for people

of good conscience to remain silent" President Thomas Jefferson

"Remember, democracy never last long. It soon wastes, exhausts, and murders itself. There never was a democracy yet that did not commit suicide." President John Adams

These were two most intelligent men ever to be President. In fact at a Nobel Peace Prize gathering at the White house President John F. Kennedy said the following to a group of scholars: "I think this is the most extraordinary collection of talent and of human knowledge that has ever gathered together at the White House, with the possible exception of when Thomas Jefferson dined alone."

We as Americans have been blessed with our forefathers knowledge and insight let's remember their tremendous contributions and not be conned by those that contribute nothing!

GOD Bless America!!

Charles S. Togias: Author Political Correctness Is Total BS

THE UNITED STATES OF CUBA 2020

(11/11/2020)

Joe Biden has been declared the 2020 President of the United States under very troubling and suspicious circumstances! A democratic society gives each person the right to vote for the representative they want to serve them. Our Constitution gives all Americans a voice and the right to choose their representatives in Washington through their ability to vote. I cannot stress this enough! It must be done fairly and without compromise. To assure our democracy this process can never be compromised. If it is it will assure the end of America as we know it.

When those advising and operating the voting booths have a self-serving agenda dedicated to changing the outcome, in favor of their candidate and are allowed to do so, we as Americans, are in serious trouble. Our entire democracy will be destroyed and if not immediately corrected America will become a socialist, communist country because many Democrats have become dedicated socialists verified by their policies. Socialism and communism are designed to suppress religious beliefs and prevent their citizens from having a voice. Webster's dictionary defines socialism as: "a system of society in which the means of production is owned and controlled by the state." In every socialist and communist country their leaders have a much more lucrative lifestyle then we the peasants they supposedly serve.

China is a great example of the treachery a socialist/communist dictatorship can inflict on the world. The coronavirus or Chinese flu as I refer to it has kill hundreds of thousands of people worldwide. The Trump administration was defeating China and bringing American companies back to America so China retaliated by causing this pandemic worldwide. I also believe this was done in compliance with billionaires, far left politicians and their media flunkies to destroy our economy to assure President Trump's removal from office. This is worldwide wholesale murder and is Hitler and Stalin like tactics. It is beyond inhumane it is murder and should be exposed worldwide and confronted. The extreme left will do anything to achieve their socialistic goals. The health and safety of humanity means nothing to them as proven by this virus.

If Biden's election is eventually confirmed and the Democratic Party wins the House and Senate 'we the people' and the America we know is in serious trouble. They would have succeeded in rigging the election, which means we will never have faith in our voting process and will implement their socialist agenda. The following is some of the things you can expect if this happens:

1. Packing the Supreme Court which will allow them to pass any and all legislation to the benefit their far-left socialist agenda. Socialism will become America's new form of government.

2. Defund the Police so when terrorists groups like BLM riot and destroy property, kill police and rob and steal from merchants in the name of the far left agenda they will have little opposition.

3. Remove the second amendment which would remove all firearms from law-abiding American citizens. Of course the criminal will not turn in their firearms as it would prevent them from their business of robbing and killing for profit.

4. Abortion will remain and will continue to destroy the lives of babies in the womb and even late term abortions will become the norm. The socialist left have even endorsed

after birth abortions. Fifty million abortions to me is America's modern day holocaust.

5. Give statehood to Washington DC and Puerto Rico assuring 4 more Senate seats which will ensure that their far left policies will never be overturned.

6. Citizenship to illegal aliens which assure a vote to the Democratic Party. Eleven million votes assure the Democrats will always control Washington!

These are just some of the policies we can expect from the socialist Democratic Party.

In Americas past our media was our assurance that there was a check and balance between Washington and the rights of our citizens. Now the media is far left and anti-Trump and the Republican Party and it borders on insanity. They jeopardize their principles for their ideology. A very simple example that cannot be denied is the Hunter Biden situation involving his father Joe and uncle. Hunter was a consultant for the Ukraine and was paid millions for his expertise. These supposedly expertise included not having any knowledge of the business he was consulting and he could not speak the language. We also found out that the Biden's have also received money from China and Russia both of which if Trump was involved in would be collusion and immediate removal from office. The main stream media said nothing!

More of the Medias credibility or complete lack of is when Hillary destroyed 30,000 emails that were supposed to be reviewed for criminal content and they said little to nothing. Also when Hillary proclaimed she was broke and then Russia put $100 million in her supposedly charitable foundation the media did not react and never investigated her for possible collusion. Every honest American knows that the media would have screamed collusion if Trump did the exact same thing? Remember after Hillary said she was broke she is now worth over $100 million and her allies in the media say nothing!

Joe Biden net worth is estimated between $30-40 million and this was accomplished by serving 47 years in politics. How could that possibly happen on a politician's salary? Barak Obama estimated net worth is estimated at $70-90 million. Hillary is a multi-millionaire as well as many more in Congress and our "honorable/righteous media" say nothing! They are too focused on condemning Trump with outrageous accusations!

What would be the Medias reaction if Trump, his

son or family was involved in any of the above?

America's media must be completely revamped and focus on truth rather than emotions and ideology. America's election process has been destroyed and unless corrected America will be the laughing stock of the world especially if we try to correct others for their misdeeds. Why in the world would any country think of America as ethically and morally righteous when we are so corrupt and divided within?

The bought and paid for media with their far left agenda is destroying America. They have got to report the news not distort the news to conform to their ideology!!

Wake up America and always defend what made us great! God Bless America forever!!

Charles S. Togias: Author Political Correctness Is Total BS

COLLUSION THAT WILL CHANGE AND DESTROY AMERICA

(11/23/2020)

In 2019 Robert Epstein was interviewed by Senator Ted Cruz, in the Senate and revealed some very damaging information that will continue to undermine and destroy America and our values if not immediately addressed and corrected. Robert Epstein is a senior research psychologist for the America Institute for Behavioral Research and Technology. Mr. Epstein a strong supporter of Hillary Clinton admitted he would never have voted for President Trump so his testimony was very creditable to me. He had no personal or political gain.

Mr. Epstein testified that the billionaires in Silicon Valley such as Goggle have the ability to change between 2 1/2 -15 million votes without ever being traced. If true and not addressed and aggressively confronted America as we know it may never recover. Mr. Epstein also said that they could have interfered with the 2016 election assuring a Hillary win but they thought it was unnecessary as they thought Hillary was a shoe in. If you question or doubt anything I am saying please go to: 2019 Robert Epstein interview with Senator Ted Cruz!

This is the main reason why I am totally convinced that the 2020 election was a complete sham. When President Trump who the media and Silicon Valley have a hatred never seen before in American history, won the election and they were in complete hysteria. This must have been what it was like with southern democrats when President Lincoln won the presidency. Hatred can overcome reason.

When we all saw the political rallies and the number of people attending it was obvious who the masses supported and it was clearly President Trump. President Trump's rallies had from ten thousand to fifty thousand at each rally while Biden's rallies numbered in the one to two hundreds and still Biden won the election. The American people were very enthusiastic for the President due to his tremendous accomplishments such as: Lowest Black, Hispanic and Asian unemployment as well as the highest stock market in the history of America. When the stock market is up and business is thriving employment goes up.

The far left, who has taken over the Democratic

Party, has a socialist agenda that if they succeed will destroy America. They have managed over many years to gain political power with a goal to bring socialism to America. To do this successfully they must remove God from America. It's like water on stone. First they removed prayer in public schools, our pledge of Alliance and remove God from the court room. Remember when former President Obama said the United States is not a Christian nation.

Now if they can gain power in the House and Senate they want to stack the Supreme Court, which will forever assure their far left agenda as well as defund police and remove the Second Amendment. Hitler in 1933 defunded police and removed guns from German citizens with his Brown Shirts which assured his demonic tranny. They will also allow late term and after birth abortions. If allowed they will destroy America and our Judeo-Christian values which has made us the envy of the world. These far left radicals want to change America forever. People like A.O.C. and Bernie Sanders who never had real jobs in their lives have now become America's leaders instead of a comedy routine!!

The left also encourages the destruction of Americas fore fathers such as Washington, Jefferson,

Lincoln and many others that were involved in making America the envy of the world. The statues of our great leaders are a form of tranny to these socialists. I asked a very simple question in my book *Political Correctness Is Total BS*: I continue to ask how many people have we ever seen crossing shark infested water going from Florida to Cuba? They all come this way and if we are so bad why are the coming here? In my home town Syracuse, NY they destroyed a Christopher Columbus Statue! What was his crime? These do nothing finger pointing far left socialist who have never accomplished a thing are always finding fault with others. Instead of being grateful living in the greatest country in the world they are always complaining and pointing fingers.

Getting back to our fraudulent election it was also revealed prior to the election, that Biden's son Hunter was involved in some very questionable and fraudulent business dealings while Biden was Vice President. Can you ever imagine what the main stream media would have done if it was Trumps son? Politicians who line their pockets while supposedly serving "we the people" should be investigated for criminal activity and removed from office not profit from the deception. This should also include their families who benefit. Biden himself along with brother and son allegedly got payoffs from China and Russia as well as son Hunter from the Ukraine. Biden has been in politics for 47 years and is allegedly worth between $30-40 million. I said in my book all politicians should have their net worth revealed prior to taking office and also revealed upon leaving office.

Remember President Harry Truman's quote: You cannot get rich in Washington unless you're a crook.

With the great enthusiasm displayed by America for one candidate and little to no response to the other as well as the criminal accusations made regarding the Biden's I thought this election was over in favor of President Trump. Especially in light of the far left socialist agenda that has taken over the Democratic Party and displayed in their approval of the riots in the democratic cities of Seattle, Portland, Chicago etc. which they described as peaceful protests I assumed that the nail was in the coffin for the Democrats. Instead there were very questionable voting irregularities in many blue states and Biden won receiving more votes than any candidate in our history. Changing votes to elect a candidate will destroy America. If Americans cannot trust the voting process, which is the foundation of our democracy then America as we know it is over.

There is an old saying don't try to con me because I was born at night but not last night!

Charles S. Togias: Author Political Correctness Is Total BS

SOCIALIST, MARXIST COMMUNIST (SMC) DEMOCRATIC STYLE

(12/16/2020)

The far left Socialists, Marxists, Communists (SMC), I do not know what title to give them that would be appropriate, that has currently taken over the Democratic Party is dedicated to destroying our capitalist Republic. This is the same party back in Jim Crow racist's southern days up to the late 1950's and early 60's that supported the evil Klu-Klux- Klan. They then and now attack and defile anyone that disagrees with their anti-American hateful agenda. Their hatred is beyond what most normal God loving people can comprehend.

Let's review who they are and their current far left committed philosophies and decide if their actions are justified or acts of extreme terror. Are they pro-American sharing our Judeo-Christian values or terrorist criminals dedicated to overthrowing America and our cherished values? We currently all witnessed a great example of this when church goers were fined and arrested for attending church because of our close proximity to others, due to the China virus but demonstrators, by the thousands, were not arrested for demonstrating and looting in the streets. In fact many of these socialist democratic politicians called these demonstrations peaceful even after stores were broken into looted and many burned to the ground. I guess it's all in the eyes of the beholder especially if they have an anti- American agenda!

Black Lives Matter (BLM) is an anti-American terrorists group that was sponsoring these riots by providing bricks a day earlier at these sites and paying people to riot. Do not let their name BLM fool you they hate America and everything we stand for. They orchestrated the tearing down of American hero's such as: Washington, Lincoln, Jefferson and Christopher Columbus and more. Their founders have terrorized America for many years and seemed to have the full support of the socialist democrats who have taken over the Democratic Party.

I believe BLM is a horrible terrorist group and their name disguises who they really are and their evil intentions to destroy America. Calling themselves BLM is marketing genius because it allows them to be thought of as a benevolent organization dedicated to helping those in need when in fact they are a terrorist organization dedicated to destroying our Capitalists Judeo-Christian society. In fact do not be surprised, as I said in my book if they inspire and lead their flock to the tearing down of Mount Rushmore. Yet the (SMC) referred to above and their billionaire anti-God supporters with the bought and paid for media are all in lock step with this plan to destroy America as we know it.

If the Hitler, one of the world's most evil people ever created would have called his group All Lives Matter they may still be destroying humanity. Don't be fool by a name; evil can disguise itself in all names and forms. Great God loving people, regardless of color condemn evil and the destruction of people and property.

Dr. Marin Luther King who I have great admiration for would never have endorsed these actions regardless of the situation. Dr. King had a turn the other cheek message and will always be my inspiration. Only evil endorses evil!

I have always thought of America as the largest most benevolent corporation in the world, **dedicated** to helping all its citizens achieve Life, Liberty and the Pursuit of Happiest through opportunity. Opportunity is the reason people from all over the world came to America. My father and his family came from Sparta

Greece when he was 9 years old in the pursuit of opportunity and he was always grateful. My father only went to the seventh grade but loved America and was grateful for the opportunities he was provided.

Now with the SMC's gaining power in the Democratic Party with the crazy members of the squad the 2020 election of President Biden and the possible control of the Senate, we will know soon, if America as the country we know and love can ever recover. Let's review the far left Washington (SMC) and review their desired agenda:

1. Defund Police

2. Remove the 2nd Amendment removing all guns from American Citizens

3. Stack the Supreme Court which will allow only far radical laws to be passed

4. Remove the Electoral College assuring only the largest states voting preference

5. Abortions early, late and after birth abortions (the legal right to destroy infants)

Let's review each of the above for its morals,

ethics and practicality and if it would benefit or hurt the average law-abiding citizen of America.

First: **Defunding Police**: we have the greatest law enforcement police departments in the world dedicated to help and serve those in need. It does not mean they do not make mistakes but it does mean the vast, vast majority are there to help us when we are in crisis. Mistakes happen especially when you are in a combat zone. They happen in the military and in the streets but they are the exception not the rule. Most police are good people and dedicated to serving. Can you imagine what America would be without them?

Removing the Second Amendment and not allowing American citizens to purchase a gun would be a great mistake. Law-abiding citizens do not commit crimes and kill innocent people only criminals do. Since the SMC's want to release many criminals from jail and groups like the BLM want to pay them to riot and destroy property getting rid of the 2nd Amendment would only put law-abiding Americans in jeopardy!

Stacking Supreme Court would allow the radicals (SMC) to take over our judicial system and America. It would be the equivalent to an American Revolution!

Removing the Electoral College would assure

all passed legislation would favor the largest states, California, Texas, New York, Florida etc. California and New York because of very poor leadership are being run into the ground and this legislation, if passed, would only compound the mess for many more.

Abortion is what I refer to as America's modern day holocaust. To have the SMC's ruling over this issue as well as the issues above is the equivalent of destroying humanity.

These are radical ideas of those that want to destroy our Constitution and our Judeo-Christian principles both of which made America the envy of the world.

I have saved the worst for the next two illustrations:

Communist China developed in its labs the Coronavirus and distributed it worldwide to kill over one million five hundred thousand innocent people with the help and planning of the SMC's. As of today it is still inflicting tremendous deaths worldwide and the end is not near! It is a Hitler type warfare that only the evilest of man-kind can inflict on humanity. With the help of the SMC's in the **United States** and worldwide they were assisted and able to inflict this pandemic and take the lives of humanity .... WORLDWIDE!! China should be closed down and have to pay trillions in retribution! They should never gain access to any industries worldwide until they pay for their evil. This was all done with many of our politician's involvement and/or looking the other way. They have sold their souls and those in our government that supported this evil or remain silent should hang their head in shame!! They will all assuredly rot in hell!

There is an old saying: You cannot negotiate with crazy people, stupid people or irrational people so do not waste your time trying. I believe these SMC's are crazy and irrational and anti-God people with an agenda to destroy America. They hate our Judeo-Christian values and have been successful, over many years at removing God from schools, from the Pledge of Alliance, the court room etc., etc., etc...

Lastly this election was the most rigged election with Biden winning in American history. If you goggle the September 2019 interview by Ted Cruz in Congress with Robert Epstein, a devout democratic supporter, who proclaimed that 2 ½ to 15 million votes can be changed without ever being detected. I knew, if true, that Trump and our democracy were in big trouble. When American votes can be manipulated, by big tech giants it is the end of our democracy as we know it. Research these far left, SMC organizations and the money that supports them and their doctrine and arrive at your own conclusions!

In my book: **Political Correctness Is Total BS**, I ask a very simple question: How many people have we ever seen crossing shark infested water going from Florida to Cuba? How come they want to come here if SMC lead countries and doctrine are so great? The evil socialist Fidel Castro's net worth was estimated at $950 million when he died. Yet to this day most Cubans, in Cuba are financially destitute while many who defected to America are flourishing. I thought the socialists were supposed to share the wealth?? I guess the socialist leaders only have to share it among themselves!

Remember America the only thing people under socialism gain is poverty-morally and spiritually!

Charles S. Togias: Author Political Correctness Is Total BS

CHINA THE EVIL EMPIRE AND ITS STEP AND FETCH IT FOLLOWERS

(1/4/2021)

The Socialists, Marxist, Communists which I will refer to as SMCs are anti-God and a threat to destroying everything moral and ethical people worldwide have stood for. They cheat, lie, steal and will destroy everyone who does not agree with their evil doctrine. They will commit acts of terror that are so inhumane that normal people with morals and ethics cannot comprehend. This was very evident with the China, coronavirus! Never forget this virus was developed in Chinese labs and spread throughout the world to kill innocence people worldwide. Only the most evil people ever created can resort to this and only those without a moral conscience can ignore it! It is Hitler like warfare!

It is a proven fact that China, a communist dictatorship did this and yet many politicians in our own country are not outraged. Many say little to nothing about this worldwide destruction of humanity. In fact many on the socialist left still blame President Trump for this devastation of humanity even though they know China was the sole predator. The left have their own version of outrage and I refer to it as selective outrage. This may have been what it was like in Germany when Hitler gained power. I know many politicians are in the pocket of these SMC billionaires and China and will sell their souls for the money and power they receive and that is a simple fact but for the supposedly main stream media to say little to nothing is very scary. Instead of exposing this destruction of humanity and those Washington politicians that have sold their souls, in the Democratic Party, the main stream media remain silent. How do they sleep at night? No amount of money can buy my principles and ethics. Corruption is corruption no matter what your political party and this is beyond corruption, its murder.

The same politicians that remain silent with the China murders are many of the same politicians that endorse by their words or silence the destruction of the statues of our founding fathers. Presidents Lincoln, Washington, Jefferson may not have been perfect but they were great men that helped our country become the envy of the world. These SMC's have even spray painted over symbols of Jesus

Christ and our places of worship and these political hacks are not outraged. America be fully aware of one thing China owns many of our self-righteous politicians. They have sold their souls for money and power but not their ability to point at others!! How do they sleep at night?

SMC mentality is anti-God and they endorsed the removal of God from our class rooms, pledge of allegiance and from our courts as well as condoning the defacing of churches and supporting the arrest of those attending church during this Chinese virus. The separation of Church and state mean nothing to them as their goal is to remove God from America! This has been their long term goal and they will not rest until America is no longer a Judeo-Christian Nation! They will rot in hell and we must never give in to their evil treachery. We as God loving Americans must always speak out for the truth and never compromise our faith.

America is the envy of the world because of our Constitution and our Judeo-Christian values and principles. The 10 Commandments gave us Gods vision for a life of love, hope and prosperity. Our Judeo-Christian values if followed are our road to a happy prosperous life. In America everyone regardless of color or financial status is a child of

God and should be treated with love and respect. I will never discriminate against color but I will always question and discriminate against behavior especially if that behavior is dedicated to violating and destroying others. If you have faith in God you will not destroy those you oppose.

Let's review the 10 commandments:

1. You shall have no other Gods before me

2. You shall not make idols

3. You shall not take the name of the Lord your God in vain

4. Remember the Sabbath day to keep it holy

5. Honor your father and your mother

6. You shall not murder

7. You shall not commit adultery

8. You shall not steal

9. You shall not bear false witness against your neighbor

10. You shall not covet

These commandments are a very basic righteous way to live a moral and ethical life. As human beings we are unable to always live by these basic rules and therefore sinful. As a Christian I know that I was not always able to live by these commandments and therefore welcomed Jesus Christ as my Lord and Savior who died on the cross to cover our sins. It is difficult to argue with any or all of these commandments especially commandment 6. That is the reason I am so upset at the Chinese virus and how and why it was developed and distributed worldwide. To purposely kill millions of unsuspecting people worldwide to gain power and money is beyond demonic. For our politicians to endorse this with their apathy or silence is also demonic.

I am sure the Biden's are not the only ones bought and paid for by China and that is very disturbing. How many others in Washington are in Chinas evil pocket? For the media not to investigate this tells me they have also sold their souls and have lost ALL credibility to anyone with an ounce of integrity!

This is why I have become such a big fan of people like Leo Terrell, black civil rights attorney. Mr. Terrell was a big liberal democrat and did not allow his opinions to be hidden. Mr. Terrell was anti Trump and way left of center until many of these revelations were discovered. Once he started to see the real truth he was unable to compromise his integrity and exposed the truth. Mr. Terrell would not compromise his principles and integrity and therefore I hold him up with honor and respect. Mr. Terrell did what most of these politicians cannot do honor truth above party!! Leo Terrell is not for sale!

America is in real trouble when we see that it's okay to murder children in the womb by the millions and now the left is endorsing late term and after birth abortions. Political candidates can be put into office by illegal voting methods performed by political criminals. A democracy is based on the majority of the will of the people and when Americans cannot trust the outcome of an election America as we know will no longer exist as the beacon of the world! I no longer have any faith in our voting process due to the far left corruption.

If these SMC can remove God from America as has been their goal over many years, America as we know it will never recover. When God is not a central part of its citizens anything goes with no consequences. I stated in my book: Political Correctness Is Total BS that a civil war may be possible in America if this anti-

God invasion does not subside. We must all stand, confront and defeat SMC terrorism!

My recommendation is to punish China by creating a worldwide boycott of all Chinese products! All products!! China will never again be allowed to sell their products anywhere in the world until they pay trillions of dollars to all those affected by the virus. This will especially be beneficial in the smaller under developed nations who have suffered greatly because of a lack of medical support. The world must stand together united against this horrible tranny to prevent a re-occurrence of this demonic human atrocity! This worldwide evil assault must never be allowed to happen again!

God Bless America and our world!!

Charles S. Togias: Author Political Correctness Is Total BS

CHARLES S. TOGIAS

WASHINGTON'S EVIL SELECTIVE CONDEMNATION

(1/13/2021)

I am watching the hearings in Washington and listening to the political outrage regarding the assault of our capital by some American citizens and I am very confused. I want to preface my forthcoming comments condemning all those that took part in the Washington demonstration that were responsible for the burning, looting and killing that took place. Six Americans died and damage was done to our capital in the name of protest. I will never condone such violence. Now as a result the political self-serving machine want to impeach our President as they blame him for the death and destruction and that is why I am a little confused.

Those politicians in Washington that are so outraged have said almost little to nothing about the Chinese virus that was developed in Chinese labs and spread throughout the world killing hundreds of thousands of innocent people and will continue to kill many more every day. I assume they were not outraged because politicians were not singled out for this assault on humanity only the masses were. These selective condemners in Washington will not condemn China for their mass murders because China owns many of them. Biden included!

These are many of the same politicians that said the riots in many cities of our country orchestrated by BLM were peaceful. In fact they never thought to bring charges against BLM and their organization. Even though thousands of stores were burned and looted and many people were murdered. Many more than the six that died and yet they were called peaceful by many democratic politicians in Washington. If they feel threatened they are outraged if the average citizen is threatened it's peaceful.

Many political hacks become multi-millionaires while their districts are in shambles. They are always pointing at their rivals and blaming them for their misdeeds. Those that par-take in this false condemnation should be run out of office and put in jail for the sake and preservation of our country. Instead they are promoted and given raises. They are the lowest of the low because they are always pointing and selectively condemning their rivals. They have not one ounce of credibility with me or anyone with a strong moral work ethic.

America you must understand that the reason China is getting away with worldwide murder is because they own many of our politicians. These political selective condemners give China the benefit of the doubt because China owns them. America be 100% assured of that and it is beyond disgraceful. Watch and see how China will gain political power within America in the next four years under the Biden administration.

China should be tried and condemned worldwide for murder. They and all their products should be outlawed worldwide until they pay trillions of dollars to all those in countries whose families have suffered from their tranny, especially those in under developed countries that lacked medical supplies to combat this Chinese self-inflicted assault on humanity. Instead these self-righteous political hacks in Washington say nothing. I guess to them it would be like slapping the hand that feeds you!

America many of these politicians will never change because they have sold their souls for power and money. Please understand they do not serve we the people, they only serve themselves and those that own them.

I had to write this article because of what I see

happening in Washington and the outrage by these selective condemners infuriates me. America as we knew it is in big trouble because of political greed. The billionaires who own Washington, along with the Chinese will do anything to change America, our Constitution and our Judeo-Christian principles. Now they are even using their high tech companies to eliminate freedom of speech. We must never allow these criminals to win.

Term limits must become the law of the land and we the people may have to take drastic measures to make this happen. I believe every man made problem has a man-made solution! America is in huge trouble and it must be addressed, confronted and solved!

God Bless America!!

Charles S. Togias: Author Political Correctness Is Total BS

COMMUNIST CHINA — THE EVIL ANTI-GOD EMPIRE

(1/25/21)

When as Americans, we witness what is happening in Washington DC it makes me think back to what **President John Adams said: "Remember, democracy never lasts long. It soon wastes, exhausts, and murders itself. There never was a democracy yet that did not commit suicide."** Many of these Washington self-righteous politicians who become multi-millionaires, by being career politicians, are in the pocket of China and special interest groups that are dedicated to Americas destruction. Their greed and selective condemnation of those they oppose are destroying the greatest country in the world. Now with their hatred for President Trump and his pro-America policies they have taken their selective outrage to new level.

Many politicians like Biden are in the pocket of China and they have diverted their attention from condemning Communist China's worldwide murdering of humanity with the development and distribution of the China Coronavirus. It is a proven fact that is was developed in China labs specifically designed to murder humanity yet these selective political condemners say nothing only focusing their selective outrage to condemning President Trump. President Trump was Chinas worst nightmare and was responsible for many US companies leaving China and returning to the United States to manufacture their products. So what Communist China, a godless government did was to develop and distribute a lethal poisonous virus and distribute it worldwide. These are Hitler and Stalin like tactics and can only be done by Godless, horrible regimes. Yet many in our government look the other way and focus on President Trump. Could it be many of these self-righteous condemners are part of the murderous plot? Remember Washington you are self-righteous if you know the horrible truth and do nothing to correct it you are the problem and as guilty as those who developed the vaccine.

Many politicians will sell their souls for power and money! **Former President Harry Truman once said: You cannot get rich in Washington unless you're a crook."** Every American must understand that many career politicians are there to benefit themselves.

Many of their districts are in shambles while their incomes continue to sky rocket. They are complete con artists only interested and gaining power and notoriety. Their support of Godless Communist China will only increase their power and money. They have sold their souls to an evil regime. They will rot in hell for their deception but until then America will crumble. Term limits are the only way America has to get rid of these horrible thieves but since they have to vote for it, it will never happen. High Tech controls our politicians and therefore Americas votes!

It's a fact that Biden and his family are in the pocket of China, as are many other American politicians and as a result they will look the other way rather than condemn China for their assault on humanity. China is solely responsible for the deaths of over one million five hundred thousand people worldwide and the numbers keep climbing and many of our politicians remind silent. They have sold their souls for power and money. China is a Communist country and has no belief in God and therefore any and all treachery on humanity goes. The problem has escalated because they are supported by big Tech billionaires who are also without God and therefore the murdering of humanity to achieve their demonic goals is accepted.

The Democratic Party which was once the party of F.D.R, Truman and Kennedy has now been taken over by the radical left. Bernie Sanders, A.O.C. and many more are changing America into a far left socialist country and our laws do not pertain to them. . A great example of this is when it was disclosed that California Congressman Eric Swalwell was having an affair with a Chinese spy and was allowed to keep his seat in the House. She worked as a fundraiser for him for years while they were dating. What do you think would have happened if Trump or one of his family members was found to have done this exact same thing? Again selective Washington outrage is the reason I have no respect or confidence in our politicians and their selective outrage.

What do these politicians gain by being career politicians and why is their character almost always in question? Let's look at three examples of politicians and how they financially benefit from serving in Washington.

1. Bernie Sanders never had a real job in his life before becoming an elected official. Please check his employment past to verify. Bernie's net worth now is estimated between 5-10 million and that might be very under reported. Check the annual salary of Congress back when

he was hired till now and try to explain how it is possible.

2. Barack Obama was a community organizer and certainly not wealthy or a millionaire before being elected President. President Obama spent eight years as President and his estimated net worth now is between 70-100 million dollars.

3. Last but in no way least of the righteous Washington insider that benefitted from Washington collusion with 80 million Big Tech counterfeit votes and is our newly "elected" President Joe Biden. Biden has been "serving we the people" in politics for over 47 years and has benefitted greatly. Biden's estimated worth is between $30-40 million again for serving "we the people." Try to checkout Biden's net worth before being elected 47 years ago, if it has not already been illegally removed by the righteous Washington criminals! Biden should be embarrassed when he points the finger at anyone for wrong doing!

These are just a few that have sold their souls for money and power! I have continually said that I want all politicians net worth to be vetted prior to taking office and after leaving office. The financial differential in numbers would staggering. This is why politician will never vote for term limits. Remembering what **former President Harry Truman said: "You cannot get rich in Washington unless you're a crook."** I cannot stress this quote enough!

This is why China will never be confronted and forced to pay for their global murders. These Chinese Communist criminals own many of our politicians especially on the left and bought their souls. Term limits are our only salvation! We must get these criminals out of Washington for America to survive.

I cannot stress enough that there should be a worldwide boycott of all Chinese products and it should not be lifted until China pays trillions of dollars to the countries and families of those affected by their evil man made virus. They knowingly spread this virus around the world to kill humanity. Only the evilest of the evil can do that and they must pay or be globally isolated forever! Those in Washington that gives China a pass and say nothing regarding these murders are as much a part of this evil as China and should be immediately removed from office.

The United States has suffered greatly but we have the resources and technology that will soon help us recover. How about these under developed countries who do not have the medical resources to overcome this Chinese assault on humanity? We should all unite to help them during their time of this evil tragedy!

Instead our political selective condemners are going to focus on the impeachment of Trump, even though he has left office to distract from their bought and paid for incompetence. China owns them and they will never hold China responsible for their global murders and that is why I have such a distain for the political left in Washington. We should throw them out of office and elect people of great integrity to replace them and to be safe and avoid a reoccurrence implement term limits.

I do not want to end this article with a negative but if we as Americans do not confront and hold big tech accountable for their voting deception we will never recover. The left is trying to remove everything related to God out of America and we must never let that happen! America is a democratic society and will only remain as such if we are able to have our votes counted fairly. The 2020 election, be assured was a complete sham! High Tech stole this election and will continue to do so in the future if not confronted and made to pay for their crimes!

Socialists, Communists and Marxists have infiltrated Big Tech, political left and the media in our country so always keep an open mind and never abandon God and his teachings!

Charles S. Togias: Author Political Correctness Is Total BS

LAWYERS AND WASHINGTON DC... CO-CONSPIRATORS IN CRIME

(2/21/21)

I stated in my book: Political Correctness Is Total BS that Washington DC is made up of lawyers and lawyers are what I refer to as being process or procedurally focused. Because, in their practice, the longer it takes them to solve a problem the more money they make. Business people, on the other hand, are outcome focused because the quicker they solve problems the more money they make. I also stated that our judicial system is designed to benefit the rich because it is based on judicial technicalities. Our political system is not a black and white system it's a rich and poor system. The wealthier you are the more chance you have of a profitable outcome. Its unfair legal distortion that can be completely manipulated by those trained in manipulation techniques. Lawyers!!!

Let me give an example. Some years ago I was

having a conversation with a judge while working out in the gym. I asked him to give me his expert judicial view on a hypothetical situation I was presenting to him. I defined the situation as follows: A judge was presiding over a trial where a criminal, with a gun, shot an innocent victim and killed him over an argument. During the trail a video was given to the judge clearly videotaping the crime. The judge saw it; the prosecutor and defense attorney also viewed it. The problem was that the video did not follow proper procedure and was therefore deemed inadmissible in court. Other than the tape there was not enough evidence to convict and the defendant went free. I asked the judge if that was justice and without hesitation he said it was 100% justice. The judge stated that this is how our judicial system works. My response was if that is how our judicial system works that means it's broken.

Defense attorneys are very well versed in how to manipulate our system to benefit themselves and those they are hired to defend. Many will use technicalities and diversionary methods to allow the guilty, they represent to avoid prosecution. They do it every day and will defend their actions as their legal right to do so. They could care less about those families that have had their loved ones criminally violated by their actions.

I am pointing this out to remind the American people of the flaws in our judicial system and the mentality of many of our politicians in Washington. A vast majority of our politicians are lawyers and think they are above those they supposedly serve. They can say or do anything to accomplish their goals while many times lining their pockets. They can and have distorted the truth of those they oppose with false testimony, hiding valuable information or misrepresenting the truth. They feel they are entitled to do so because of their legal upbringing. Anyone with strong principles, morals and ethics could never justify these actions. We would never be able to sleep at night!

These self-righteous political, selective condemners, as I refer to them, are ruining the United States of America. Former President Trump, who these far left Washington politicians hated, was a victim of their hatred. Trump could never have gotten their approval, even with his many great accomplishments for the benefit of the American people because they are not interested in the American people they are only interested in themselves, their personal gains and the billionaires they serve. Billionaires own them, the media and their political party.

I keep stressing that America is in big trouble because these anti-God billionaires own the far left politicians and our media. Many of our politicians have sold their souls to line their pockets and will do anything including letting these far left paid for protesters remove God and our Judeo-Christian values from America. These politicians say nothing when our forefather's statues are destroyed and our churches and statues of Jesus Christ our Lord and Savior are defaced. America was the envy of the world because of our belief in God and his teachings yet our bought and paid for politicians in Washington remain silent. They have sold their souls to tranny!

I wrote this article to emphasize how America is being attacked and dismantled from within. I will never stop voicing my condemnation regarding these criminals as my principles cannot be bought and silenced at any price! We as God Loving Americans must never remain silent when you see our great country being attacked and compromised!

Thomas Jefferson one of Americas greatest Presidents said:

"All tranny needs to gain a foot hold is for people of good conscience to remain silent"
Charles S. Togias: Author Political Correctness Is Total BS

WASHINGTON'S RIGHTEOUS SECULAR OUTRAGE A COMPLETE CON-GAME

(3/8/2021)

Many of our Washington elected officials and their billionaire big tech supporters are doing everything possible to change America into a secular anti-God country. I have said many times in my articles that these billionaires in and out of big tech own the media and too many of our politicians. They have a well thought out plan to destroy America by removing many of our traditions as well as our Judeo-Christian values and drastically change our Constitution. Their plan is brilliant because they continue to use what I have referred to as a water on stone type philosophy, very hard to detect until it's too late to confront.

Many of our politicians have sold their souls for power and money. They will do whatever their told if the price is right. As I have repeatedly stated in previous articles the closing of our places of worship due to the pandemic and the close proximity to others, punishable by arrest was justified by these political criminals in Washington due to the pandemic. Yet they said nothing about the criminals rioting by the thousands in the streets and in fact described these riots as peaceful demonstrations. They will distort the facts to and make their political points to those they serve and because they do not have a moral compass anything goes.

What is happening on a day to day basis should frighten all Americans who love America and our democracy. Because of these far left socialist and their day to day efforts to destroy America and our values I cannot remain silent. I will continue to expose them and their evil deeds. I will not remain quiet and they cannot pay me enough to compromise my principles. Remember theses billionaires own these political swamp rats in Washington and they will do anything they are told to do. As I have said many times they have sold their souls. I refuse to do so!

Now, believe it or not, these self-righteous swamp rats in Washington have turned the other way when these anti-America groups like Black Lives Matter and others are attacking Americans and our scared traditions. These far left anti-God groups in America own many in Washington. They have gone as far as attacking many of our traditions. Names of sport teams, food products, tearing down of our heroic forefather's statues and the attacks on our churches and even the statue of Jesus Christ are being destroyed.

Now these self-righteous America anti-God haters who will look under a magnifying glass to find and expose America's faults have gone to a ridiculous new low by attacking the Dr. Seuss books. They want them removed from book shelves for their racist's imagery. It's beyond crazy but true. Here are the books they want removed:

1. And to Think I saw it on Mulberry Street
2. If I ran the Zoo
3. McElligots Deal
4. On Beyond Zebra
5. Scrambled Eggs Super
6. The Cats Quizzer

These books to the self-righteous anti-God finger pointers are a complete attack on America and our values. Let me see if I got this right, the Doctor Seuss children's books along with professional sports team names and food products, the crazy anti-God left want outlawed because they are disrespecting a minority of Americans. Yet these same far left socialist say nothing about rap music that attacks women and encourages and glorifies crime and murder of police and those of a different race.

How about the complete show of disrespect many of these multi-millionaire athletes demonstrate when they kneel for our national anthem? They show complete disrespect to all of our military, many of whom died and or were crippled for life, to defend them and our nation from tranny. They are never criticized for their complete disrespect by the finger pointing left. Remember those in the military they are disrespecting make minimum wage!

When BLM rioted and destroyed businesses and killed an injured many Americans that was considered a peaceful demonstration and not a threat to America, but these fictional cartoon books are a threat to these self-righteous finger pointers. They are beyond hypocrites; they are dangerous anti American revolutionaries. They will find fault with everything in our glorious history.

I will never stop exposing them and their anti-God and anti-American revolutionary war on America and our traditions. I have used quotes from some of our greatest leaders to prove my point over and over again. I have written many articles because we as Americans must understand this far left attack if not confronted and defeated will destroy America.

Remember America the 2020 Presidential election was a complete fraud and should be a wakeup call to all of us. If we cannot trust those who are in charge of counting the votes during a national election who can we trust?

Charles S. Togias Author Political Correctness Is Total BS

CHARLES S. TOGIAS

COMMUNIST? MARXIST? SOCIALIST? DEMOCRATIC PARTY!

(3/11/21)

"Remember, democracy never lasts long. It soon wastes, exhausts and murders itself. There never was a democracy yet that did not commit suicide." President John Adams said this as a warning to our politicians and to our citizens as early as the seventeen hundreds. Warning them that we should not take our wonderful democracy for granted. I wanted to start this article with this quote because what the far left politicians in the Democratic Party are doing, if successful, will change America forever! Many of them are owned by anti-God billionaires who are dedicated to changing America.

America all we have to do to verify my deep concerns, is to look at what has happened and what is happening to America before our very eyes. First we experienced a Chinese virus that was developed in Chinese labs that has killed over two million people worldwide with no end in sight and our so called democratic leaders in Washington will not address this travesty by confronting China and demanding that they pay trillions of dollars to mankind all over the world. Until this is done China and all their products should be banned.

Only Communists, Marxists and Socialist countries can inflict this damage to humanity because they are without God and therefore anything goes regardless of the causalities. Yet our so called leaders remain silent. China not only owns Joe Biden , his brother and son they own many in the democratic party and that is why they look the other way to this attack against humanity.

We have all witnessed the far left selective outrage against President Trump as they have tried to impeach him twice for, what they say are violations of our American traditions. How do these selective condemners describe their violations? Yet they say little to nothing about China and their murdering of millions of people. Congressional representative Eric Swalwell of California has been dating a Chinese spy and our Congressional representatives remain silent. I wonder why? Could it be you do not criticize the hand that feeds you? Representative Swalwell is a joke and should be thrown out of Washington for his association with a Chinese spy yet he is rarely if ever confronted.

The corruption and deception does not end there

it's only the tip of the iceberg. We now have a new President elected with smoke and mirrors technology. Remember as I have stated in other articles that it's not as important who votes it's much more important who counts the votes especially now in America where big tech has taken over. I want to continue to go on record as saying the 2020 Presidential election was a complete sham and anyone that is principle centered knows that.

In previous articles I asked my readers to go and check out a 2019 interview with Senator Ted Cruz and Robert Epstein where Mr. Epstein stated that 2.5-15 million votes can be changed without being detected. After what all Americans witnessed at the voting sites all unbiased thinking Americans know that the 2020 Presidential election was a complete fraud and Joe Biden is not our President.

As I continue to voice my concerns with how the far left is undermining America and all our Judeo-Christian values as well as our Constitution I must focus on other areas of great concern. I will list them in bullet form to be able to cover as many as possible. Get ready America!

- Packing the Supreme Court which if successful will allow them to make their far left anti God agenda a reality. All their legislation, that I believe is a very socialist agenda, will be assured to be passed to America's democratic destruction.

- Removing the Second Amendment which will remove all guns from law-abiding citizens similar to what Adolph Hitler did in Germany which allowed his brown shirts to take over the government. Criminals will never turn in their guns so unarming law-abiding citizens will only create more crime.

- Allowing illegal entry into our country, including criminals which the corrupt politicians can use to receive votes. The far left politicians know that they will receive a huge voting majority that will vote for those that enabled them to come to America as well as all the illegal votes.

- Washington DC as well as Puerto Rico becoming states because this will guarantee the Electoral College vote.

- Abortions with no restrictions. Late Term and after birth abortions will allow any and all abortions to be legal. I have and will continue to refer to late term and after birth abortions as America's modern day holocaust. Fifty million innocent infant deaths are beyond demonic to everyone but the non-believing Communist, Marxist, Socialists!!

- Now Americans are having their votes

compromised by big tech and these billionaires that own them. Remember America if we cannot trust the voting process America as we know it is over.

Last but not least: We have politicians in Washington describing the Black Live Matter terrorist group as conducting peaceful demonstration even when they are burning down stores, attacking innocence people, killing police while arming their followers with bricks and guns. These politicians and those that fund them are very dangerous to our great country.

I love good people of all colors and one of my favorite American hero's was Dr. Martin Luther King. Dr. King was an inspiration to all and his non-Violent protests I will never forget. When he talked he was very uplifting and fought for equality for all. I see many people of color that are great Americans, like Leo Terrell, Larry Elder, Hershel Walker, Thomas Sowell, Candace Owens just to name a very few. They have great integrity and love America and will never compromise their principles.

Throughout my book the reader will be able to feel my frustration with our politicians in Washington, many who have sold their souls for money and power. The Far Left is trying to destroy our history and integrity. They are trying to compromise and falsify our Forefathers, Constitution and Judeo-Christian heritage. Their vision for America, if successful will be complete devastation and corruption.

As I stated I was in the advertising business and to successfully communicate your message you need both reach and frequency. Reach is the number of people who hear the message and frequency is the number of times they hear it. As you could tell when reading my book I use frequency to bring clarity. I don't think you will ever wonder where I stand.

I hope you enjoyed my book and do not remain silent regarding Americas future!

Charles S. Togias, Author, *Political Correctness Is Total BS*

AUTHORS RECAP

America is being attacked from within by anti-God forces dedicated to changing America into a secular society void of any spiritual influence. As I have said in my articles this attack has taken place over many years and was a calculated, well thought-out strategy designed to remove God and his teachings from American society. The Socialist, Communist, Marxist, to be referred to as (SCM) have removed God and prayer from public schools, our Pledge of Allegiance as well as in our swearing in ceremony in the court rooms. This was done over many years and is a water on stone type of warfare that is not evident until it's too late.

We witness terrorist organizations like Black Lives Matter (BLM) rioting in the streets of American and many socialist democrats described these riots as peaceful demonstrations. As I have stated many times the only credible thing about BLM is their name. Their hatred and actions tell the true story as to who they are and their diabolical intentions. They are dedicated to destroying America and everything we stand for. Look up their founders!

BLM have bricks delivered to so call peaceful demonstration sites a day before the demonstrations and the media say nothing about this. These bricks are delivered so their so called peaceful demonstrators, many of them paid for by BLM, can cause harm, death and complete destruction to these demonstration sites. Yet many of our bought and paid for politicians have proclaimed that these riots were peaceful demonstrations and their media flunkies agree with them. They have sold their souls for money and power.

At the same time as these riots are taking place the far left Washington, put money in my pocket, politicians told us we can be arrested for attending church. They stated because we were at risk due to the virus and our close proximity to those attending. Let me see if I got this straight: You can demonstrate in our streets by the thousands and not be arrested for being too close and destroying people and property but cannot go to your place of worship without the fear of being arrested? In fact many in Washington said these horrible riots were peaceful demonstrations. When someone lies to you once and you believe them it's their fault. When they continually lie and miss represent themselves and you believe them it's your fault. The far left politicians and main stream media are bought and paid by anti-God billionaires and have sold their souls.

This 2020 Presidential election was a complete fraud and anyone with an open mind knows it. There was no enthusiasm for candidate Biden and yet he got the most votes ever recorded in American history. With all the violations of voter fraud at the voting sites and so many non-registered voters and dead people's ballots being counted there should have been a complete investigation and our media said nothing. I wonder what they would have done if the exact same thing happened and Trump won. I was very leery prior to the election when I saw a 2019 interview by Senator Ted Cruz and Robert Epstein, a democratic supporter, on google predicting that 2.5-15 million votes can be altered without ever being detected. Remember if you do not have God in your life any and all deception goes.

America we are just witnessing the tip of the ice berg now that our fraudulent election has enabled the socialist far left communists (SMC) to enter our country with a goal to destroy our democracy. The 2020 election and the infiltration by the left will bring America down if not confronted. We, as God loving Americans must stand and confront and expose their evil philosophies. We must never give into these anti-God attacks. Our children and our children's children must never be exposed to this evil.

Americans know without a doubt that Communist China developed the Coronavirus in their medical labs and distributed it throughout the world to murder innocent men, women and children. There have been over two million deaths worldwide and the numbers keep growing at an alarming rate. Biden, his family and many of our politicians are bought and paid for by China. I am certain that this is the main reason the election was fixed because our politicians do not want their cash cow to be exposed and penalized! This is demonic tranny, Washington style, at its lowest level.

Warning to America and the world if China can indiscriminately murder millions of human beings worldwide over a loss of businesses and create this virus they are capable of anything and have no regard for human life. China, in my opinion is very capable of starting World War III! China is an evil Communist Dictatorship and any and all methods to dominate the world are within their vision! As Americans we must never remain silent or complacent to evil and we must never give into tranny!

President Thomas Jefferson said: "All tranny

needs to gain a foot hold is for people of good conscience to remain silent."

That's why I will never stop writing these articles as long as these anti-God and anti-America haters have an influence over our democratic process and lives. They are trying to destroy our wonderful history and those of our brave forefathers. They have torn down statues of Presidents Jefferson, Lincoln and many more American heroes. They even damaged churches and images of Jesus Christ my Lord and Savior. So America when you see this evil stand strong and never condone it because the evil SMC's are dedicated to destroying everything we stand for.

President Abraham Lincoln said: "This nation will remain the land of the free only so long as it is the home of the brave."

AUTHORS BIO

Upon returning from service in Vietnam I spent the majority of my career in media sales and sales management and was fortunate enough to spend a vast majority of that time working for WSYR, an NBC affiliate located in Syracuse New York. Over my career we were owned by Newhouse Broadcasting, later Katz Communications and then employee owned by New City communications. All great companies are dedicated to their employee's growth and success and they were. I cannot thank them enough!

They provided us with the best corporate trainers in the world. Example: Herb Cohen who negotiated with Iran, during the Carter administration, for the release of our embassy personal trained us in negotiation techniques. At the time Mr. Cohen was considered by Washington as the best!

After leaving the media I took my skills and created a Leadership, Sales and Marketing Consulting company, Step 2 Training Systems with clients in the United States and Australia. My business book entitled Create Loyal Customers in an Unloyal World defines my system from start to end. I always believed that great companies emulate the functional family. The functional family was the most effective and efficient group ever created. Because they love, teach and discipline those they lead.

Many years ago I created 5 elements that enable great leaders to become role models and a valuable resource to those they lead. These are defined in my book.

1. **Role Models:** will never ask those they lead to do anything they wouldn't do. They lead by example. Always on time, well dressed with a positive uplifting attitude. "Your attitude, not aptitude determines your altitude."

2. Improve the skills and behavior of those they lead: Great leaders are always looking to improve themselves and improve the skills of those they lead. They are judged by how those they lead help others and improve their situations.

3. Discipline non Performance: To improve performance you must identify and discipline poor performance. Great leaders must never over look or excuse poor performance.

4. Motivate through recognition: Because great

leaders must confront and discipline non-performance they must always recognize and celebrate a job well done. If leaders only find fault without celebrating successes they will drain their team of its energy. I always recommend that great performance must be celebrated as a team.

5. Strategists: are always meeting with their team and reviewing success and failures with the ultimate goal of continually improving performance. Sun Tzu said: "it is that in war that the victorious strategist only seeks battle after victory has been won." In other words victory is won before the battle is fought through planning and strategies.

- 1963-65 Attended Onondaga Community College Syracuse, New York

- 1966 Parsons College Fairfield Iowa January enrollment (Basketball Scholarship)

- September 1966 drafted

- 1967-68 Military service Vietnam

- 1971 joined NBC affiliate WSYR A/F sales staff

Syracuse, N.Y.

- 1978 Promoted to General Manager 17% revenue share in 21 station market

- 1982 sales team revenue increased to 40% share

- 1986 sales team revenue share 55% #1 nationally for small to medium market

- 1992 left media business and created Step 2 Training Systems-Corporate Leadership, Sales and Marketing Consulting System. With clients in US and Australia.

I believe we are made up of body, mind and spirit and as a result I have always tried to include improve and stimulate all three. I wrote 3 books in my mid to late 60's, to stimulate my mind and I pray every day, many times per day for my spiritual growth. For my body I work out at the gym three times per week. I do 180 chin-ups 3 days/540 per week and over 28,000 chin-ups per year as well as weight training. At age 70 I did 630 chin ups in 2 hours, 12 minutes and 19 seconds.

Because I came from a functional family with a

strong father who disciplined non-performance and a loving mother and live in the greatest country in the world America I believe if it is to be it is up to me!